MOUNTAIN GORILLA IN A CENTRAL AFRICAN FOREST
FOLLOWING PAGES: GREAT EGRET ON SANIBEL ISLAND, FLORIDA

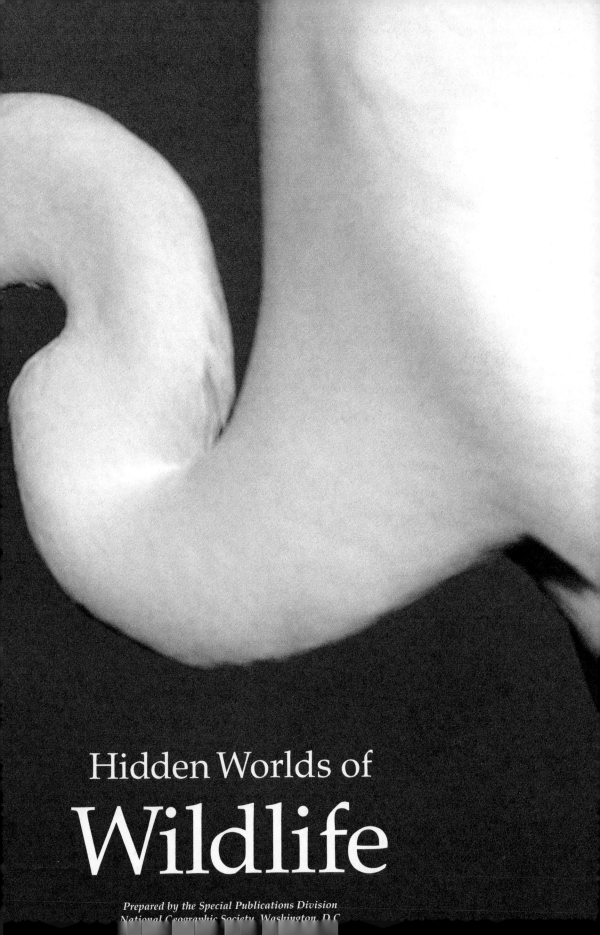

Hidden Worlds of
Wildlife

Prepared by the Special Publications Division
National Geographic Society, Washington, D.C.

HIDDEN WORLDS OF WILDLIFE

Contributing Authors: Christine Eckstrom,
Ron Fisher, Kim Heacox, Thomas O'Neill

Contributing Photographers: Robert Caputo,
Bill Curtsinger, David Doubilet,
Stephen J. Krasemann, Michael S. Yamashita

Published by The National Geographic Society
Gilbert M. Grosvenor, *President and
Chairman of the Board*
Melvin M. Payne, *Chairman Emeritus*
Owen R. Anderson, *Executive Vice President*
Robert L. Breeden, *Senior Vice President,
Publications and Educational Media*

Prepared by The Special Publications Division
Donald J. Crump, *Director*
Bonnie S. Lawrence, *Assistant Director*

Staff for this book
Margery G. Dunn, *Managing Editor*
John G. Agnone, *Illustrations Editor*
Viviane Y. Silverman, *Art Director*
Victoria D. Garrett, Alice Jablonsky,
Jacqueline N. Thompson, *Researchers*
Catherine D. Hughes, *Contributing Researcher*
Philip B. Silcott, Toni Eugene, *Consulting Editors*
Richard M. Crum, Christine Eckstrom,
Tom Melham, Thomas O'Neill,
Gene S. Stuart, *Picture Legend Writers*
Jody Bolt, Susan I. Friedman, Joseph F. Ochlak,
Map Research and Production
Sandra F. Lotterman, *Editorial Assistant*
Sharon Kocsis Berry, *Illustrations Assistant*

Engraving, Printing, and Product Manufacture
George V. White, *Director,* and
Vincent P. Ryan, *Manager, Manufacturing and
Quality Management*
David V. Showers, *Production Manager*
Lewis R. Bassford, *Production Project Manager*
Timothy H. Ewing, *Assistant Production Manager*

Carol R. Curtis, Rosamund Garner, Karen Katz,
Lisa A. LaFuria, Katharine N. Old,
Dru M. Stancampiano, Marilyn J. Williams,
Staff Assistants

Lucinda L. Smith, *Indexer*

*Turret eye of a Jackson's chameleon swivels
in search of insects. This tree-dwelling lizard
is native to East Africa.*

J. B. DAVIDSON / SURVIVAL ANGLIA

4

Contents

EUROPE

ASIA

AFRICA

PACIFIC
OCEAN

Etosha N.P.
①

INDIAN
OCEAN

Papua
New Guinea
⑤

③

AUSTRALIA

New
Zealand
③
Doubtful
Sound

ANTARCTICA

McMurdo
Sound ③

Habitats featured in this book range from African savanna to subarctic wilderness, from tropical forest to polar sea.

FOLLOWING PAGES: A green sea turtle swims in Pacific waters off Costa Rica.
M. MOISNARD / JACANA

Foreword

HIDDEN WORLDS OF WILDLIFE celebrates some wonderful places and some marvelous and strange creatures. I know well most of the tropical locales featured in the book, and as I scan its elegant pages, I find myself reliving memorable times in Costa Rica, Guyana, Micronesia, New Guinea, and eastern and southern Africa. I have not been to the Yukon, but I have heard its call. I still have yellowing paperback editions of Robert Service's ballads of the Yukon, read and reread during long winter evenings in Northern Ireland 30 years ago. Yet their message was compelling rather than inviting, and I never went. We turtle biologists find that our work calls us to the tropics more than to the frozen north.

Wildlife, for the most part, is indeed hidden; concealment is an essential component of survival for both predator and prey. It takes someone as daring as Bill Curtsinger to follow penguins under the Antarctic ice; as patient as Chris Eckstrom in her blind at Etosha to witness the primordial predator-prey interactions of Africa; as persistent—and well-guided—as Ron Fisher and Mike Yamashita to find the incredible birds of paradise in New Guinea. I spent two months in Papua New Guinea myself once, on a sea turtle mission, but I saw no birds of paradise until my last morning in the country, when I was taken by a new friend to a spot only an hour or two west of Port Moresby. By 9 a.m. we had seen Count Raggi's, king, and twelve-wired birds of paradise; the magnificent riflebird; and the glossy-mantled manucode. But I would have seen none had I not been shown exactly where to look.

Yet occasionally wildlife can be seen in its splendor without special skills. The great sea turtles, for example, can be seen by anyone willing to wait for them on their nesting beaches—although, as Tom O'Neill relates, the duration of the wait may be unpredictable. But whether it be a single leatherback emergence or an arribada of tens of thousands of olive ridleys, the reward always justifies the wait.

Chris Eckstrom's thrilling final vision of Africa brings to mind the most dramatic wildlife tableau engraved on my own memory. It was on my third safari to Kenya—and on my wife's first night in Africa. Exhausted from travel, we retired early at Kilaguni Lodge in Tsavo National Park, but something prompted us to wake and open the curtain around midnight. At the water hole a hundred yards away, under a full moon that illuminated the far hills, were a dozen or more elephants, forty Grant's zebras, and, approaching from the right, a vast herd of hundreds of Cape buffalo. The great beasts moved slowly and were almost silent, and their calm was awe-inspiring. Scenes such as this convince the conservationist, amateur or professional, that his strivings to preserve the wilds of Planet Earth must never cease.

Peter C. H. Pritchard
Florida Audubon Society

WILDLIFE WORLDS:

A Portfolio

*Its wings
spanning six feet,
a northern gannet
airlifts seaweed
for nest building.
The gannet's world
encompasses
the rocky cliffs of
Bonaventure
Island off
Canada's Gaspé
Peninsula, where
these seabirds nest
in the thousands.*
JEAN MICHEL LABAT / JACANA

*FOLLOWING
PAGES: In Florida's
marshy Everglades,
an American
crocodile displays
a behavior called
mouth gaping,
which may
help regulate
body temperature.*
STAN OSOLINSKI /
OXFORD SCIENTIFIC FILMS

Death grip proclaims a jaguar the victor over a young black caiman in an Amazonian rain forest. Expert swimmers, jaguars wade into water to capture prey. Black caimans, South America's largest predators, feed on fish, other reptiles, and mammals as big as calves.
LOREN McINTYRE

14

Hanging like a hammock, a three-toed sloth cradles its baby in a rain forest in Panama. These slow-moving mammals spend almost all their lives in trees. Their shaggy fur serves as camouflage, blending with the tangled foliage.
MICHAEL FOGDEN

PAGES 18–19: In Alaska a red fox pup dashes about with a meal from its mother— a freshly killed ground squirrel.
© STEPHEN J. KRASEMANN / DRK PHOTO

Winged angler, a bald eagle swoops over Alaska's Chilkat River in pursuit of salmon. Long imperiled, this majestic raptor now thrives chiefly in remote wilderness areas.
FRANK OBERLE

FOLLOWING PAGES: *Acrobats of New World rain forests, spider monkeys swing through the treetops. Anchored by its prehensile tail, one drinks from a balsa flower.*
MICHAEL FOGDEN / OXFORD SCIENTIFIC FILMS

Etosha:

Dry Season Oasis

*Glowing nimbus of light surrounds
an elephant tossing arcs of
dust to coat its hide for protection
against the fierce African sun.
Beyond stretch the bleached flats
of the Etosha Pan, a vast prehistoric
lake bed and the hub of life in
Namibia's Etosha National Park.
Some 50,000 big mammals roam this
parched wilderness reserve
covering more than 8,500 square
miles in the interior plains
of southwestern Africa.*

ANNIE GRIFFITHS BELT

Text by Christine Eckstrom
Photographs by Robert Caputo

T he lions last roared just before dawn, booming black thunderheads of sound into the night, their calls so long and loud and resonant they seemed to rumble through the earth and roar back from the moon. Then they softened and fell, mournful and low, like a moan for the pain of the land. It is the heart of the dry season on the interior plains of southwestern Africa. No rain has fallen for more than six months; no clouds sail the skies. It will be another month or more before mountains of white cumulus build up on the northeast horizon, and the water they eventually bring may not be enough, again. The last good rain that soaked the land fell ten years ago. The grasses are straw-dry, thickets creak, the winds exhale dust, the land cracks. Everything—every mopane tree whose brittle leaves whir in the gusts like locust wings, every animal whose eyes gleam from the dark screen of woodlands beyond the lions—everything thirsts.

Sunrise comes and two eagles soar through pastel skies high above, surveying the expanses of savanna woodlands and grassy bush that stretch for flat miles in every direction. They may not see me far below, hidden inside a blind, or the lions I've been watching, now deep shadows in the shade of an acacia tree, but they spy the round pool of water between us, an artesian spring twinkling blue in the center of a small, bare plain. Later, the eagles will come to drink there, as will an array of big mammals little rivaled for variety of species in any other part of Africa: zebras and springboks, red hartebeests and giraffes, impalas and gemsboks, kudus and elands, blue wildebeests and warthogs, hyenas and jackals, and still later, in darkness, breeding herds of elephants and rhinos with calves. All day and night I'll see them emerge from the woodlands, easing to the water that most must drink daily to live. All will be wary—and aware that beneath the acacia tree the dozing lions that prey on them probably know exactly where they are.

The spring where I'm camped lies near the vast dry lake bed in north-central Namibia known as the Etosha Pan. It is a remote and undercelebrated corner of the continent, a sere region that, especially at the brutal peak of the dry season, looks so bleached and inhospitable it seems little life could survive there. But the water shining before me is part of a system of springs along the southern shore of the Etosha Pan that transform the land. They are the only perennial natural waters for scores of square miles in every direction—magnets for animals of every size and stripe. Along with the unique water cycles of Etosha's ecosystem, the springs enable the near-desert terrain around me to support an overflowing ark of wildlife.

The Etosha Pan and an immensity of wild land around it are protected within the fenced borders of Etosha National Park, administered by the government of Namibia. Covering more than 8,500 square miles—an area greater than that of the state of Massachusetts—it is one of the largest national parks in the world. Some 50,000 mammals, ranging in size from jackals to elephants, roam the park, including about 300 black rhinos—10 percent of all the black rhinos remaining in the wild. I came to Etosha to explore the wildlife realms the park preserves, returning often to the blind by the spring, in daylight and darkness, to witness the pageant of animals. I came also to consider the relationships between landscape and wildlife, especially Etosha's big mammals.

There are as many visitors to Etosha each year as there are big mammals in the park, and, like most people, photographer Bob Caputo and I arrived in the dry season, which extends from about May to December. Although it was for both of us a first journey to southern Africa, the wildlife seemed familiar. Most of Etosha's big mammals and those of southern Africa's grassy plains are similar or identical to species found in East Africa's savannas, like the animals of Tanzania's Serengeti National Park and Kenya's Maasai Mara—places I have visited several times on safaris and where Bob has both worked and lived. The resemblance is more than coincidental, for the distribution of wildlife in eastern and southern Africa today is tied to ancient earth movements and climatic changes that contributed to the rise and spread of the mammals we had come to Etosha to see.

Though less well known than the parks of East Africa, Etosha is more intensely managed for tourism as well as for wildlife. The park is patrolled by scouts on foot and on horseback and by rangers in four-wheel-drive vehicles. Animals are counted and monitored by wildlife researchers, and a fence 500 miles in circumference encloses the entire park to discourage animals from straying onto adjacent farmlands. Although Bob and I traveled around Etosha in two four-wheel-drive trucks, the roads open to visitors can be toured (Continued on page 42)

FOLLOWING PAGES: Dry season blooms of Acacia nebrownii *offer browse to an elephant. It may have broken its tusk in a jostling bout at a water hole, where elephants often compete to drink at the spring's source.*

Animal tracks crisscross the surface clay of the Etosha Pan, bone-dry except in the brief rainy season. Nearby, a young elephant bathes in one of the perennial springs fringing the 1,800-square-mile pan that enable Etosha to sustain a wealth of wildlife year-round.

FOLLOWING PAGES: A typical elephant herd, probably consisting of two family groups, approaches a water hole.

Ears flared in aggression, a young elephant chases away a group of zebras from a water hole. Elephants often display such intolerance for the presence of other species at springs. Tempers fired as if by the heat, male zebras (opposite) battle for dominance near a water hole.

PAGES 36–37: Zebras and springboks drink peaceably at one of Etosha's permanent alkaline springs, where a great array of animal species congregate in spectacular numbers during the long dry season.

Near the pan a mother zebra nuzzles her young. When a herd takes flight, it looks like a blurred swirl of stripes — possibly a defense mechanism that confuses predators.

FOLLOWING PAGES: *Rare creature, rarely seen, a black
rhino edges along a spring. Critically endangered, only
3,000 black rhinos remain in the wild; 300 live in Etosha.*

by car. And while we sometimes used our vehicles as mobile camps when we joined researchers and rangers in remote areas, we returned between trips to a home base at one of the park's three well-provisioned tourist camps along the southern shore of the pan.

But management and amenities can be deceptive; Etosha belongs to the animals. The park's three camps are small clearings in a wilderness, encircled like frontier forts by stone walls and wire fences, their gates closed each night to keep animals out and people safe inside; I often awoke to hear lions roaring just outside the wall by my bungalow. During the day it is we who look out from the windowed cocoons of our vehicles to experience something increasingly rare in Africa and elsewhere: the sights and scents and sounds of animals living wild.

The nucleus of the park is the Etosha Pan itself, an oblong lake bed covering nearly 1,800 square miles. Composed of clay and alkaline mineral salts, it is a saline desert, level and barren and painfully white in the sun. From afar, the pan looks like the sea, sometimes silvery blue in the glare of high noon, when the air above its surface is so fluid with visible heat that it seems great currents of water are flowing over the pan. Animals wandering out on its flats—a lone gemsbok, scattered ostriches, a line of loping giraffes—appear to rise above the horizon and walk through clear air, afloat in a shimmering mirage. Even in darkness the pan can be seen, moon-white in a land of black shadows, as if the heat that poured down from the sun all day had generated a pale light within the pan, making it glow through the night.

Animal tracks vein the pan, leading far into its white interior. From the water holes along the shore, animals retreat to the pan's empty expanses, where an approaching predator has no cover. One evening I watched as a herd of wildebeests moved away from a spring and out onto the pan, dark beasts on an ivory desert, trudging in long jagged lines, heads low, until they vanished over the horizon into the night. Two days later near the same spring I found the remains of a fresh wildebeest kill, the story of a young animal's misjudgment and a lion pride's success recorded in tracks on the pan.

Seen up close, the pan's expanses are crunchy with paper-thin bubbles of clay or crackled into raised hexagons so fragile and sunbaked they crumble to powder underfoot. Throughout the dry months each track in the clay is preserved like a fossil, and the surface of the pan is inscribed with a season's worth of passages and dramas—meanderings and pursuits, sudden endings and escapes, even brief visits by people like me—until big bruised thunderheads swell over Etosha and the tracks and their tales are slowly erased by the rains.

Although sometimes they fail and often they're fickle, the annual rains set the tempo of life in Etosha. If they arrive as expected, beginning around January, within days grasses sprout, flowers bloom, trees leaf, and Etosha's savannas and woodlands become a wild garden of greenery. From the springs by the pan, animals scatter around the region to graze fresh pastures and to drink from sweet pools of rainwater sparkling across the plains. "When the rains come," the park's chief conservator, Alan Cilliers, told me, "the wildlife literally moves out overnight. Today you'll see hundreds of animals drinking at a water hole, and tomorrow you won't see a tick."

Rainfall in Etosha averages only 12 to 18 inches a year, and the lush times are brief. Grasslands and pools quickly dry out, the green patina fades. After three or four months the vanished animals gradually reappear from the withering land, drawn back to the permanent pinpoints of water around the pan.

If you could read the animal trails that groove the park, they would tell a story of the seasons and migrations of Etosha. Tracks radiate from each water hole like the spokes of a wheel, leading from spring to pan and plain to woodland, forming a crazed tracery throughout the park. The densest webbing of trails connects the vital water holes along the southern shore of the pan, as does a network of gravel roads built so that visitors can travel from spring to spring, following the herds of wildebeests, zebras, springboks, and others as they move steadily to the east in the dry season and westward with the rains.

Every water hole is a stage for wildlife dramas, and during the dry season animals and animal watchers alike are concentrated at the springs, where small signs in English, German, and Afrikaans advise: "Patience will be rewarded." People park by the water and wait. Most of Etosha's animals are so habituated to people in vehicles that they completely ignore them, but what you are privileged to see is largely a matter of luck. You may sit at a water hole all day, as I have done, and watch a pride of lions with empty bellies sleep while wildebeests graze nearby. Or you could chance upon a startling scene, as Bob Caputo did one day, when a leopard leaped down from a tree to seize a springbok—and dragged it away between parked cars full of visitors.

At first I roamed Etosha like a nomad, finding places to sit in solitude, taking pleasure in the simple beauty of particular animals and scenes. Forty elands wind through high golden grass, dewlaps swinging, and disappear one by one—like ghosts through walls—into a forest of mopane trees. Out on the pan in the noonday heat, two male zebras trot out from a herd and rear up to fight, dancing on hind hooves, nipping each other's necks. On the edge of a woodland by a secluded seep, a rhino rubs its cheeks and flanks against a stump, and flops down to wallow in a mud hole. A flurry of dainty springboks races across the road, then "pronks" in joyous stiff-legged leaps over the open plain. I remember the easy confidence of the leopard that walked out from thick bush by a spring, swatted at a sand grouse as if it were a fly, then strode down to drink, lapping loudly, eyes on me—a perfect portrait of predator bravado.

I always stopped and stared longest when I saw the elephants; their very presence seems to dignify the places they walk. The largest land animals on earth roam Etosha—and Africa, where they still can—

like a physical measure of the grandeur of the land. One afternoon I followed a breeding herd of ten, led by an old matriarch, as it headed west through parched bush—seven adult females easing forward in ever shifting combinations, mesmerizing in the heavy grace of their motions, with three young ones racing to keep pace with them, seeking shelter among the temple columns of their mothers' legs. Here and there they all paused to graze—tearing up bunches of dry grass, curling it up to their mouths, ears flapping, heads turning—then moved forward again, marching steadily as if on a mission.

Then, single file, they crossed into the road and stopped. Standing against a huge tangerine ball of setting sun, facing me less than ten yards away, they began scooping up trunkfuls of dust from the road and blowing it above their heads, through their legs, and over their backs—a coat of protection for their hides against the relentless heat of the sun. Trunkful after trunkful, in thickening brown clouds, great geysers of dust filled the air, the elephants tossing it up in high fans and swirling scarves, powdering their silhouettes, bending and swaying in halos of sunlight and dust.

So ethereal did the elephants appear that I would have believed they possessed some sense of their own aura of mystery, of the effect of the scene they created, as they slowly turned together and walked out from the dust and into the savanna, moving westward again, and faster now, into the darkening bush. Later that night I understood the reason for their determined course when I found them again, ten miles to the west, gathered at a spring where they must bring their young daily, all drinking deep drafts of water.

The springs so essential to life in Etosha owe their existence to both the annual rains and the peculiar nature of the region's geology. Much of the land surrounding the pan is calcrete, a limestone deposit formed by the evaporation of underground water over time. Some of the springs are artesian, flowing up from deep in the earth through porous limestone hillocks. Others occur in natural depressions that cut into the high water table, while the springs at the very edge of the pan arise where rainwater absorbed by the calcrete seeps out onto the pan's impermeable clay. Though alkaline and bitter, the springs are all the animals have for the eight or more rainless months of the year.

The tone of life in Etosha in the dry season is taut, a feeling dictated as much by the animals as by the bare-boned look of the land. Sooner or later nearly every animal must go to a water hole, or thirst and die. But prey animals also sense the threat of death that lurks at the springs. Predators know that the animals will come to the water, and they lie in wait for them there. Of Etosha's big mammal predators—lions, leopards, cheetahs, and hyenas—it is the lions that are the boldest and most dominant. They will take over kills made by other big cats and by hyenas. Jackals, while hunters themselves, usually scavenge the scraps from lion kills, waiting nearby until the lions walk away, sated. I once found five cheetahs, a mother and four young, hunched in a tight circle around a springbok they had just killed on a plain near the pan. They ate quickly but were so uneasy that rarely did all five feed simultaneously; one or two were always looking around, anxious, heads raised high, necks craning—and I realized that the cheetahs, formidable predators in their own right, were scanning the edges of the plain in fear of lions.

Where the lions are and what they are doing shapes in many ways the behavior of most of Etosha's other big mammals. Even the simple question of whether or not the lions look hungry or ready to hunt seems to ripple through the air like a rumor. I found that I thought of the lions every day, though I might not see or hear them at all, and wondered whenever I stopped at a spring if they were hidden somewhere near me in the bush, watching.

I f you sit alone with animals and observe them long enough, you can get lost in their worlds, and part of the wonder of being among them is the slow-dawning feeling for a sense of their lives, an imagined view through their eyes. One day I stopped at a spring on the edge of the pan frequented by a large pride of lions. It was deserted when I drove up, but soon the animals began to arrive. First came a family of four kudus, parents and two young, the great spiraling horns of the male polished with sunlight as he looked around slowly, scanning the bush, stepping cautiously down to the water, his family close behind him. Then a dozen more kudus appeared, followed by a long chain of zebras, heads nodding, tails swishing, with a lone gemsbok bringing up the rear. Three giraffes approached from the pan, accompanied by two ostriches and a small herd of wildebeests. Then springboks stepped forth from the bush, as elegant and long-legged as Thoroughbred colts. One after another came the springboks—40, 50, then 60—with one kori bustard in the middle of their line, striding in perfect synchrony with the springbok parade as if trying to sneak in and pass unnoticed.

But all the animals were nervous and became more so as they neared the water. They stopped every few steps to look around and eased in so slowly that it took most of them more than an hour to reach the edge of the spring. When they did, they paused long and stared hard—ears perked, muscles tensed—before bending their heads down to drink. All are most vulnerable then, especially giraffes, which must splay their front legs and bend their knees deeply before they can lower their heads to the water. Often, it is at that moment, when the animals are drinking, that the lions charge.

Inside the truck I found myself absorbed in the animals' fears, glancing over my shoulders, searching the bush for a flick of an ear or a flip of a tail that would betray the cover of a lion. Though I could not see them, it seemed that the lions were near. Watching the animals and projecting myself into their individual worlds, I came to feel their tension so keenly that when a dove suddenly flew up from the water's edge, startling the gemsbok into a leap that spooked all the other animals and set them to flight, I jumped in my seat and (Continued on page 54)

45

Speaking "trunk language," young elephants engage in a friendly embrace, behavior common among members of the same group and between separate herds. Traveling in family groups, elephants range across Etosha, as they once did over all of Africa. Some herds, though related, may not cross paths for years, but their remembered ties endure, reaffirmed in simple greetings like the twining of trunks.

After a near-fatal drink, two springboks narrowly escape the explosive charge of a lone lioness (opposite, top and above). Most animals disperse when a pride comes to drink (left).

FOLLOWING PAGES: Panting in the heat, a young lion guards the reward of his hunting prowess.

During courtship, a lion tests the air for
a female's scent. He grimaces with a teeth-
baring gape known as flehmen behavior to
detect the breeding readiness of a female.
Lionesses and their cubs, like those at left, form
the permanent nucleus of the pride—
a structure that helps ensure the reproductive
and hunting success of the only social cats.

accidentally hit the horn, ensuring the end of activity at that spring for the rest of the afternoon. I never did know if lions were there just then, but when I returned to the spring the next morning, a pride of 23 lions lay sprawled on the ground, lolling and drowsing, with evidence of their kill still on their faces and paws.

On other African plains, such as Tanzania's Serengeti, the dry season brings lean times for all the animals, including lions. The great herds are spread far apart then, in search of the last decent places to graze, but when the rains green the central plains of the Serengeti, the animals congregate there in the millions—and the lions feast. In Etosha, the situation is reversed. The lions grow fat in the dry season, when the predictability of prey animals coming to water holes makes hunting easy, but when the rains come and the animals scatter, the fortunes of some prides change. The territories they define with their roars and defend against other prides—sometimes to the death—may be suddenly empty of prey; they may have to fight other lions to follow the moving herds. Research in Etosha suggests that the pride structure so crucial to the lions' hunting success may break down then, and some lions become nomads with no fixed territory to claim, growing thin in the season of plenty. But with the onset of the dry months they return, like the herds, to the springs by the pan, to roar out their territories anew, to crouch by the waters and wait.

G eographically, the Etosha Pan is both the lowest point of a huge inland basin and the heart of an ecosystem that reaches far beyond the park's broad borders. At the Etosha Ecological Institute in Okaukuejo, site of the park's headquarters and main tourist camp, chief biologist Dr. Malan Lindeque gave me a large-scale overview of Etosha.

"The Etosha ecosystem has been long overlooked and underrated," Malan said. "In actual fact, it is one of the great phenomena of Africa, and recent work has shown that it's an even more intricate and beautiful system than we had previously imagined." We spread maps of Etosha, southern Africa, and the continent across his desk for a telescoping look at the land over time, beginning in the early Miocene epoch, some 24 million years ago. "Much of the continent was relatively low and level then," Malan explained, "and the interior of southern Africa, from what is now Zaire down to the Cape, was filled with a massive sedimentary basin. Then came millions of years of geologic upheavals, when the Great Rift Valley and most of Africa's mountains and lakes were formed. What's left of the original superbasin now is the Kalahari Basin to the east in Botswana, and the Etosha Basin, which extends from here north into Angola."

We focused on a map of southern Africa. "Thousands of years ago," Malan continued, "Etosha was a much wetter system. The pan was a lake, and we used to think that it dried up when earth movements diverted the course of a tributary that brought water to the pan. But new studies have shown that this river probably never fed the pan. Etosha has slowly dried up because of long-term climatic changes over the past 10,000 years or so. The whole continent has been slowly drying out through this period—and it's probably going to get even drier."

The rhythms of Etosha are more subtle and wondrous than the story suggested by the theory of a diverted tributary. The ecosystem really begins more than 200 miles north of the pan in the central highlands of Angola, source of a small river known as the Cuvelai. Swollen by annual rains, the river flows south toward Namibia, where Angola's mountains give way to the flat expanses of the Etosha Basin stretching for hundreds of miles to the south. There the Cuvelai's waters fan out into a network of shallow waterways, or *oshanas*, that wind lazily through the seasonal swamps of Ovamboland just north of Etosha. Gradually the oshanas gather together and flow into a depression called Lake Oponono; from the south side of the lake a single river, the Ekuma, emerges and leads down into the Etosha Pan.

In rainier times gone by, Etosha was replenished each year by the floods from Angola, flowing down the Ekuma into the pan. "In most years now, the waters from the Angola highlands don't even reach the pan," Malan said. "Sometimes the Ekuma River fills right up to its mouth and doesn't have enough force to enter the pan. But in a year of really exceptional rainfall—perhaps once a decade—the waters do flood in, and the Etosha Pan itself, this completely barren environment that otherwise supports virtually no life whatsoever, changes from a desert into an oasis."

When it floods, the pan becomes a gigantic blue lake nearly as large as the state of Delaware, teeming with schools of barbel and tilapia, with countless masses of bullfrogs and turtles just emerged from estivation. Great flocks of white pelicans, storks, and waterfowl wing in from all over southern Africa, and pink clouds of flamingos—sometimes numbering more than a million—soar in from the coast of Namibia and from East Africa's Rift Valley lakes to nest in the pan's briny shallows.

In years past, before fences completed in 1973 enclosed the park, land animals around the region lived by the complex clockwork of Etosha's ecosystem. "It's almost impossible now to find out Etosha's former magnet range for wildlife," Malan explained, "because so little research had been done before they started building the fences in the 1950s—and Etosha was first seen by Europeans just over a century ago. We do know that this was a vital dry season refuge for animals from all over the Etosha Basin, but there may have been longer-term cycles in some animal movements as well. It's possible that wildebeests migrated here from the deserts to the east. During the drought of 1979 to 1983, 2,000 Hartmann's zebras from the mountains to the west trekked down to the park for water, and elephants from all over broke through the fences and came in. But as soon as the rains arrived, they left."

Elephants, the great wayfarers among land mammals, once wandered over the entire African continent. They are of abiding interest to

Malan; Etosha's elephants were the subject of his doctoral thesis, and he continues to study them both within and beyond the park, finding intriguing evidence of where they go and of the relationships that exist among elephant groups throughout the region.

"Elephants will always try to go their own way regardless of what humans do," Malan said. "Although they move with the seasons for water and food, there are places elephants may go every year or once a decade or even once in their lives for reasons we do not understand. Still, those places are a part of their overall life range and of their network of contact with other elephants."

Etosha's elephants and other big mammals have had to survive on scantier resources and in a more marginal habitat than have their kinfolk elsewhere in Africa. "The quality of elephant ivory is poorer in Etosha," Malan told me, "and the tusks are shorter. I'm analyzing the mineral composition of ivory here to see if our elephants are almost permanently on a starvation diet. But I've got a theory about their short tusks that I'm busy testing. Elephants in Etosha fight at the water holes, sparring to get the best position at the outlets, and they break their tusks there. I've got hundreds of ivory chips collected from the areas around the eyes of the springs, where the freshest water trickles out."

Although the size and quality of their tusks may make Etosha's elephants less desirable to the ivory hunters who have decimated elephant populations all over Africa, protection of wildlife in Etosha has been exemplary for a continent where poaching, especially of rhinos and elephants, is highly organized, lucrative, and insidiously widespread. The last of the earth's wild black rhinos number a mere 3,000—a total population that would fill an area the size of three football fields—and hunters in the African bush are stalking them now. Etosha alone holds 300 black rhinos, more than are found in any other reserve, and if vigilant park policing continues, the rhinos there may have a chance. In recent years the number of elephants in Etosha has actually increased—there are now several thousand—and I recall the statement on their status implied in a telling observation Bob Caputo made. He has photographed elephants often during his years in East Africa, and one morning in Etosha he found an old bull that had recently died. "I've seen a lot of elephant carcasses in my life," he remarked, "but this is the first one I've ever seen with tusks."

Etosha is one of the few places in Africa where you may see elephants and rhinos together in the wild. Although in the daytime elephant breeding herds and rhinos are so shy that they seldom visit the springs, both must drink, usually daily, and they often come to the water holes under cover of darkness. One afternoon before the full moon rose, I drove to the blind by my favorite spring near the pan to watch for elephants and rhinos, and to observe the world of the African night.

The wildlife blind had been recently built, a roofed platform overlooking the spring, with hinged screen flaps around the sides and an open doorway reached by a ladder with 14 steps. It seemed obvious and exposed, but I had been there several times before, and the animals had walked by the blind as if it had been a tree, while up inside I had enjoyed the illusion of being invisible and omniscient.

I parked my truck near the blind, carried my gear up the ladder—and noticed that the giraffes, zebras, and wildebeests that were drinking at the spring when I arrived had suddenly vanished. Standing in the doorway, I scanned the woodlands ahead through binoculars, then glanced down and saw the reason for the animals' disappearance: two huge male lions, strolling right by the ladder, looking up at me.

They walked to the spring and crouched to drink, so near that I could hear huffs of breath as they lapped. They were as big as any lions I had ever seen, and listening to them drink I found their presence changing my behavior as much as that of the animals now hidden in the woodlands. I worried about the blind's open doorway and about the incentive the lions might have to climb up. With the truck too far away for me to reach, I decided on a tactic of silence and stillness—and hoped that the lions would not smell my fear.

One finished drinking and lay down by the water; the other walked toward the blind. He stopped, scratched a patch of ground, marked it, then flopped down in the dust, looked up at me—and roared. Then the second lion roared and they roared back and forth, over and over and ever louder, with sounds so great they vibrated the blind—and me—as I crouched unmoving.

After sunset the lions moved to the other side of the water, rolled over on their backs, legs in the air, and fell asleep. The sky blackened and the moon rose higher, illuminating the white stones that strew the plain like stars fallen to earth. Then, along the southern edge of the woodlands, a dark form moved, and as it neared the spring, I saw the great horned profile of a rhino. Two more rhinos, a mother and her calf, eased in from the west, and the lions continued to sleep as all three rhinos bent to drink beneath a sky lit so brightly by the moon that they touched noses with their reflections in the water. When they finished and left, as quietly as they had come, their moon shadows followed them across the plain, where they merged into the trees.

Moments later two breeding herds of elephants appeared, striding majestically onto the plain along parallel trails, trunks raised high in question mark shapes, testing the air for danger. The lions sat up and roared. Lions will take rhino or elephant calves if they can, but they rarely do—the mothers can attack and kill lions in defense of their young. The elephants paused, trunks up, sniffing the lions, then formed a closed ring around the pale pool, protecting their calves as they all drew long trunkfuls of water, tilting their heads back to drink— a nodding circle of massive gray beasts with tusks as white as the moon.

Just after midnight a third herd of elephants trumpeted from the south and entered the plain at a run. They were a breeding herd of 15, bold and aggressive, led by an old matriarch. Ears flared, she headed straight for the lions, flinging trunkfuls of dust at them. The two big cats slunk away, tails low, to lie by the edge of the woodland.

For more than an hour the elephants drank and bathed and frolicked in the moonlit pool, sometimes sloshing the water back and forth with their legs and submerging themselves in the spring; one blew bubbles with its trunk. Then, strangely, one by one the elephants moved away from the water and over to the place the lion had marked near the blind. Huddled in a tight circle, they began kicking the ground and stirring the dust—stubbing toes at the earth, scuffing front legs back and forth—and with their trunks they began scooping up small mounds of dust, curling it to their mouths, seeming to taste it, then tossing it away like spoiled food. For half an hour they shuffled in the lion's dust, scooping, tasting, discarding, and stamping again, softly rumbling to one another as they steadily obliterated the mark of the lion. Then, abruptly, the old matriarch stopped, turned, and walked toward the woodland, with the others stepping away to follow her in a head-to-tail line until they all disappeared, leaving soft clouds of dust in the air behind them and a great circle of platter-round prints on the ground where the lion had lain.

The lions returned and sat down by the water together, alert but silent now, as two shapes emerged from opposite sides of the woodlands and slowly moved to the spring—a solitary rhino easing up to one side and an old bull elephant to the other. They faced each other as they bowed to the water, two venerable gray creatures of the continent, with the lions resting between them, eyes closed, shaggy manes hoary with moonlight. It was a primordial vision of Africa, a secret gathering of animals in the night, but so otherworldly under the luminous sky that it seemed like an image from an ancient memory, and I accepted it for my own as a gift from the animals.

An hour before dawn a last herd of elephants arrived, trumpeting wildly, and hyenas on opposite sides of the plain began to whoop. Then jackals joined in from all around the woodlands with long, rising cries, like keening women inconsolable with grief. The lions raised their heads and roared one last time into the African wilderness.

Now in the season of thirst their roars are bold and resound over all. But soon, when the rains come and ring like chimes calling animals out to the distant savannas, the lion's roar will sound like the voice of hunger, moaning for the dry season to bring the herds back to the small blue eye of water on the plain near the pan.   □

Collective gaze of a trio of giraffes betrays their wariness near a water hole, where even the world's tallest animals walk in fear of lions. Giraffes are especially vulnerable when they splay their front legs and bend low to drink.

Leopard's patience yields an
unusual daytime kill of springbok
(right)—an event made even more
surprising by the presence of
wildlife watchers in vehicles parked
near photographer Bob Caputo.
More than 50,000 people travel to
Etosha each year. Though some
animals, like the springbok pair
nibbling an acacia (above), seem
used to human visitors, spectacles
of life in the park are entirely wild.

PAGES 62–63: In the wake of
departing lions, a jackal fights
with vultures over the leavings
of a wildebeest carcass.

Hazy expanses of the Etosha Pan shimmer in the heat as a gemsbok and her calf stand amid sparse grasses of

a near-desert land. Perpetual springs and just enough rain
make this dry corner of Africa a wildlife paradise.

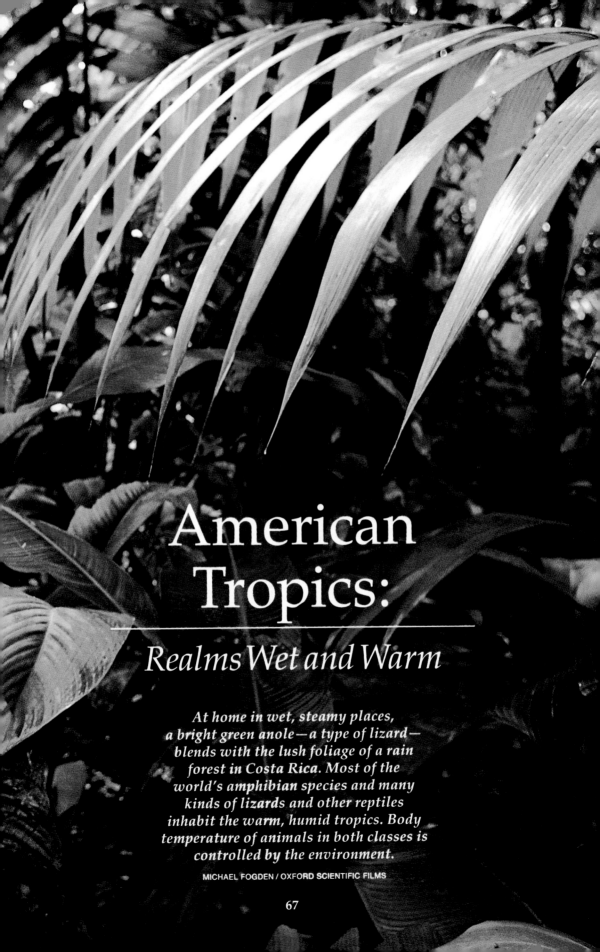

American Tropics:

Realms Wet and Warm

At home in wet, steamy places,
a bright green anole—a type of lizard—
blends with the lush foliage of a rain
forest in Costa Rica. Most of the
world's amphibian species and many
kinds of lizards and other reptiles
inhabit the warm, humid tropics. Body
temperature of animals in both classes is
controlled by the environment.

MICHAEL FOGDEN / OXFORD SCIENTIFIC FILMS

Text by Thomas O'Neill

A creature of the light, I quickened my steps along the darkening forest path, the night fast on my heels. High in the canopy, where the last wisps of daylight were snagged, monkeys appeared to hurry as well, a pack of them noisily trapezing through the treetops, using their prehensile tails as grips. On the forest floor a covey of tinamous—plump, quail-like birds—faded into the tangled undergrowth, their high-pitched murmurings suspended in the humid air. I bent down to marvel at a procession of leaf-cutting ants, hundreds of them moving single file like a chain gang, neatly clipped shards of vegetation held above their heads. When I looked up, I saw only darkness.

Night had fallen with tropical abruptness on the Costa Rican rain forest. As if on cue, rain began to drum harshly on the leaves. Nearly 160 inches falls yearly here in La Selva, a 3,700-acre research station in northeastern Costa Rica. As the rain thickened, other sounds pierced my consciousness. From afar I heard a muffled roar, almost as if the night, like a territorial beast, was proclaiming its dominance. Switching on a flashlight, I began to move cautiously toward the noise, following a rain-splattered cone of light into the mysterious dark.

The volume rose and rose until I stepped into a wet clearing, a swamp, and the din enveloped me. I doused the light and listened. The sounds began to separate themselves. From the blackness of the forest came the shrill, deafening rasp of katydids, the sound of countless insect wings rubbing together. Against that wall of noise other sounds emerged—whoops, squeaks, meows, chirps, clucks, an ethereal *tink tink tink*. It was a hullabaloo of frogs.

I sprayed my light across the swamp—which only hours before had been dry and seemingly deserted—and discovered everywhere the noisy amphibians. Pale-yellow tree frogs, no larger than my watch dial, had stationed themselves on the broad leaves of *Spathiphyllum* growing profusely in the swamp waters. Each time a frog called, the vocal sac under its throat inflated and its entire body pulsed. La Selva researchers liken the sound to the squeaking of wet sneakers.

Cluck cluck. My light followed this call and pinpointed at the base of a tree one of the most spectacular of all tropical amphibians—the gaudy leaf frog, *Agalychnis callidryas,* whose scientific name means "beautiful tree nymph." Large for a tree frog, the two-inch-long creature was arrayed in flamboyant costume-party colors—brilliant green back, purple sides with creamy white stripes, dark blue legs, orange feet, and bulging red eyes. Cluck cluck, indeed. Its flashy colors are likely meant to startle predators, giving the long-legged frog time to leap away.

My presence did nothing to quell the hubbub. The vocalizing frogs, all of them males, were single-minded: They were calling for mates. The conditions were right—a warm, rainy night—and the females appeared obliging. As the night deepened, I noticed more and more frogs mating, the males stolidly clasping the backs of the females with their forelegs. In most frog species the male fertilizes the eggs externally as the female lays them; they hatch into tadpoles after a period ranging from a few days to a few weeks, depending on the kind of frog and the environment.

While investigating a tree for frogs, I found a leaf dripping with a gelatinous blob of eggs, fully formed tadpoles visible inside, ready to hatch and fall into the water below to begin their aquatic life, which ends with their metamorphosis into froglets. Heaps of white foam dappled the water; these were floating nests, churned up by the hind feet of male leptodactylid frogs. A foam nest protects the eggs and keeps them moist. The shallow water itself, having reappeared during the last few hours of rain, teemed with newly hatched tadpoles and with frogs liberated from the dry leaf litter.

If the swamp is a hothouse of fertility on a wet night, it is also a hunters' paradise. In the forest pond voracious aquatic insects and small fish preyed on tadpoles and freshly laid eggs. Bats swished overhead. A large brown spider had snared a yellow hylid frog and was sucking out the body fluids. An orange snake was coiled on a damp leaf, looking as if it had all night to wait for an imprudent frog. Another reptile, a cat-eyed snake, had wrapped its slender tan length around a branch to feed on eggs beading the bark. The frogs kept calling. The night was their stage.

Night—unilluminated night—will forever remain a foreign realm to us light-loving humans. Darkness, with its disembodied sounds and impenetrable depths, puts us at a natural disadvantage—we can't see. We should be sleeping. For many of the world's 6,500 known species of reptiles and most of the 4,000 known species of amphibians, however, the coming of night signals a renewal of activity. Under night's dark mantle, scaly reptiles and moist-skinned amphibians emerge to hunt, feed, and breed.

To search for amphibians and reptiles and learn about their ways in the New World tropics, I became a denizen of the night myself—pacing starlit beaches in quest of nesting sea turtles, following frogs' calls down dark forest trails, paddling an equatorial river at midnight to observe stealthy black caimans, large crocodilians. *(Continued on page 80)*

Denizen of the tropical forest, a red-webbed tree frog waits for a mate. Its raised, protruding eyes allow the low-slung amphibian to spy prey and predator alike. Sticky foot webbing and toe disks provide a firm grip. On rainy nights the shrill chorus of male frogs calling for mates reaches a crescendo.

MICHAEL FOGDEN

Parenting frog-style finds a male glass frog guarding the female's spawn. Eventually tadpoles will hatch from the soft, jelly-encased eggs and fall off the leaf into water. Unusual among frog species, the eggs of the rain frog (above) produce completely metamorphosed young.
MICHAEL FOGDEN (BOTH)

Cat-eyed snake
emerges at night
to feast on frog
eggs. The frogs
themselves are
hunted after dark
by bats, spiders,
and snakes.
MICHAEL FOGDEN

FOLLOWING
PAGES: Looking
death in the eye,
a huge marine
toad assumes a
defensive stance
before a toad-
eating snake. The
amphibian's
highly toxic skin
secretions deter
most predators.
MICHAEL FOGDEN

*Intent on prey, an eyelash viper establishes a lookout
post in the fronds of a palm tree. The venomous snake
takes its name from an enlarged scale above each eye. The*

"lashes" may protect the eyes of the viper as it slithers along vines and branches. Heat-sensing pits on both sides of its head enable it to locate prey in the dark.
MICHAEL FOGDEN

For my nocturnal sleuthing I traveled to Costa Rica, a Central American country blessed with a remarkable diversity of amphibian and reptilian life. It is home to nearly 130 known species of frogs and toads, and many thousands of sea turtles of several species nest on beaches along both its Pacific and Caribbean coasts. An exception in the tropical world, Costa Rica has established a system of national parks and nature reserves, totaling almost a fifth of its land area, to protect its natural bounty. I also journeyed to Guyana, a small South American country that has some of the continent's finest untouched wilderness.

Most amphibian species and many reptilian ones live in the humid tropics for the simple reason that these regions are wet and warm. The warmth is crucial because the members of these two ancient classes of vertebrates are ectotherms; that is, their body temperature is controlled by the temperature of their surroundings. The steady warmth of the tropical rain forests, where thick vegetation and high humidity hinder heat from escaping at night, allows amphibians and reptiles to easily maintain their body temperature.

The wetness of the rain forest particularly benefits amphibians. Normally not inclined to drink water, most of them require moist surroundings so that water can be absorbed through their skin. Their shell-less eggs, a legacy of fish ancestors, also require moist conditions—hence the great egg-laying activity of frogs on rainy nights.

A nocturnal life-style suits amphibians because most of them would not survive for long in the direct glare of the sun. They would roast and dry out, given the permeable nature of their soft skin. Most amphibians spend the daylight hours under cover—hidden beneath leaves, rocks, and logs, burrowed in the ground, or immersed in tiny oases of rainwater at the center of bromeliads. Their skin normally maintains its moistness through mucous secretions, which give the animals their characteristic sticky or slimy feel.

Tough, scaly skin permits snakes and other reptiles to bask for hours in sunlight. They regulate their body temperature by moving between sun and shade. Some reptiles, particularly crocodilians, move into water at night since water retains heat longer than land does. Water-dwelling turtles often lay their eggs at night, thereby avoiding exposure to the sun and also escaping the notice of many predators.

Wet, dark, and warm—these are ideal conditions for a host of amphibians and reptiles. The tropical night consequently has millions of eyes—those of frogs, toads, salamanders, snakes, crocodilians, lizards, and, as I was to discover in spectacular fashion, sea turtles.

My search for sea turtles got off to an exotic false start. One early July I rendezvoused with British-born conservationist and turtle expert Peter Pritchard in Guyana's steamy capital city of Georgetown, and together we set off for a remote Atlantic Ocean beach near the Venezuelan border, on the northern coast of South America.

"Almond Beach is a special place," Peter said. "It may be the only beach in the world where four species of sea turtles nest together—hawksbills, half-ton leatherbacks, greens, and olive ridleys, now on the verge of extinction in the Atlantic."

Almond Beach edges a trackless forest that extends for hundreds of miles before giving way to mountains and savannas. Its isolation pleases Peter, who haunts the tropics worldwide to study turtles. Exhibiting that peculiar zest for the difficult and the uncomfortable that inveterate British travelers often have, Peter dismissed the option of chartering a plane and instead mapped out a land and sea route. We ended up taking two and a half days to go 150 miles. We traveled by taxi over cratered coastal roads; hired a boat to ferry us across the broad, island-strewn mouth of the Essequibo River; and were marooned for 30 hours in the village of Charity because of a nationwide fuel shortage. Villagers asked Peter if he had come up-country as part of a malaria treatment team. "No," the sun-reddened visitor replied, straightening his tall frame. "I've come to save turtles."

For the final leg of our journey we took to the open ocean, bucking and pitching over the continental shelf in a leaky wooden boat. The unvarying coast—a green wall of mangroves and occasional yellow strands of sand—looked no more real than a heat mirage when viewed for hours through blowing salt spray. We finally came ashore near four thatched lean-tos—the camp at Almond Beach.

"The first time I landed here, I was greeted by a dozen turtle poachers," Peter recalled as we climbed out of the battered boat and into the warm, silty surf. "And here was the greatest poacher of them all."

"Hello, Doctor Peter," said the short, powerfully built man with mahogany-brown skin who stepped forward and with polite formality shook our hands. He was Audley James, an Arawak Indian from the village of Santa Rosa. For years Audley and his fellow villagers had been ambushing sea turtles here, removing eggs from nests and killing the mother turtles. The eggs and meat became seasonal delicacies to the Santa Rosa Indians. Now the same Audley James angrily chases poachers into the mangrove swamps. In a startling transformation he'd become Doctor Peter's loyal accomplice, committed to saving sea turtles.

Having known for years about the sea turtle carnage on Almond Beach, Peter, now a vice president and field biologist of the Florida Audubon Society, resolved to find some solutions when he journeyed to the South American coast in 1987. His ties to Guyana stretched back to 1964 when, as an Oxford undergraduate on holiday, he made the first documented report of a ridley turtle nesting in what was then British Guiana. In 1971 he married a Guyanese woman and now considers himself to be at least spiritually a Guyanese.

Lugging a slide projector, screen, and small generator, Peter visited Indian villages along the coast to spread the gospel about sea turtles: Here were marvelous creatures that have been around for 90 million years, ever since they abandoned land for water; seven of the eight species are threatened or endangered throughout their range; and if the

81

exploitation for meat, skin, and tortoiseshell continues, then someday no turtles will climb your beaches. The slide shows and the preaching worked. Chastened and inspired, Audley James agreed to head a camp of several fellow Arawaks, mostly members of his family, who are paid a small salary to defend Almond Beach against poachers during the nesting season, from March to August. They also keep detailed records of the turtles' shore calls.

"I can't imagine killing a turtle now," Audley told me in his missionary-school English the first night we patrolled the ten miles of nesting ground. "Peter made us understand that the turtles were disappearing. Now I am so close to them."

The program has been an impressive success. During the first half of the 1988 nesting season, up to five or six turtles were being illegally slaughtered each night. You can find sun-bleached turtle bones and shells scattered like driftwood in the morning-glory vines above the high-tide line. With Audley and his relatives as guardians of Almond Beach, turtle kills dropped to ten for the entire 1989 season.

For four nights I trod the crushed-shell beach with the Arawaks and with Peter, who visits the camp from time to time each nesting season. We used our flashlights sparingly; most nesting turtles are skittish, and a sudden show of light may make them abort a nesting attempt. Our eyes strained to pick up any slow-moving dark shape or the scuff marks of a flipper-dug trail. Female sea turtles return to land only to dig nests and lay eggs; males may never leave the water. Other than a few species of snakes, sea turtles are the only fully marine reptiles.

Given their brief, clandestine appearances on land, it's little wonder that mystery still shrouds the behavior of sea turtles. Walking a pitch-black tropical beach night after night gives you time to ponder some questions about them. For instance, where do baby turtles spend the first years of their lives? Few have ever been seen. Scientists guess that they feed in protective pastures of seaweed such as those of the Sargasso Sea in the North Atlantic. How are some turtles able to navigate prodigious distances? Green turtles inhabiting the coast of Brazil undertake journeys of 1,400 miles to nest on Ascension Island in the middle of the South Atlantic. Do turtles return to their natal beaches to nest? No tag has stayed on a hatchling long enough for scientists to monitor its pelagic roaming.

But to me the most pressing mystery of all was: Where were the turtles that nest on Almond Beach? After Peter's buildup, I was stunned that only a single turtle—a hawksbill, and an unseen one at that—had ventured out of the water in a week's time, the longest such hiatus since the Indians began keeping records. After a while I sensed that we all felt a bit lonely marching up and down the coarse sand at night with no turtles on which to lavish our attention. We found no nocturnal poachers either. During a beachcombing excursion one afternoon, three of us did surprise a pair of scruffy fishermen with machetes slung from their belts. They looked ready to dig into a leatherback's nest. We nervously sized up the odds—we had the numbers, they had the weapons—but the two men played innocent and accompanied us back to camp for a drink of rainwater.

Our last night on the beach, Peter waded into the surf and tasted the water. "It's fresh," he announced. Peter theorized that a shift in the prevailing currents had temporarily rerouted the massive freshwater discharge of the Orinoco River in Venezuela so that it was now flowing south along the Guyanese coast. The change in the salinity of the off-shore waters, he guessed, was disrupting the turtles' nesting behavior. We ended up staring silently out across the dark ocean. The night persisted in keeping its secrets to itself.

Sea turtle searches can run to extremes, from walking along stifling, mosquito-infested beaches all night and finding nothing, to stepping onto cooling sand at twilight and within minutes being surrounded by more turtles than you can count. I know, because three months after getting skunked in Guyana, I showed up one sultry October day in the village of Ostional on the Pacific coast of Costa Rica and there was implored by young children to, quick, run to the sea and look at the *tortugas*. Light was draining from the western sky when I reached the wide beach, but I could see well enough to know that I had struck the naturalist's mother lode.

Advancing from the sea, crawling up the beach, feverishly digging nests were hundreds and later thousands of olive ridley sea turtles. So abundant were they that the mobbing of their dark, wet shells in the surf zone made the lower beach appear as if it were cobblestoned. A haze hung over the area from all the sand being flung into the air by the digging reptiles. Louder, more insistent than the waves were the *thump thumps* heard all around as 80-pound turtles vigorously rocked their plastrons, or ventral shells, on the sand, smoothing down freshly covered nests with their hind flippers. Darkness came and the number of ancient-looking armored reptiles swarming ashore only multiplied. I felt as though I had wandered into the middle of a sci-fi movie: *Invasion of the Shell Creatures.*

I was witnessing an *arribada* (Spanish for "arrival"), the mass nesting emergence of the olive ridley, surely one of the most spectacular examples of group activity in the animal kingdom. Over five nights, an estimated 157,000 ridleys came ashore. With an average of 107 eggs to a clutch, that meant almost 17 million eggs buried on a half-mile stretch of beach. Afterward, the beach looked as though army maneuvers had been held there; it was all chewed up by the digging and the crawling. The stench of exposed, rotting eggs rose into the sweltering air. The turtles had made sure no beach resort would ever be planted there.

The olive ridley of the eastern Pacific and the Indian Ocean and the closely related Kemp's ridley of the Gulf of Mexico and the North Atlantic are the only two species of sea turtle to display such large-scale collective behavior. Major arribadas occur in only five places in the world:

two in Costa Rica (on Playa Ostional, where I went, and on Playa Nancite in Santa Rosa National Park to the north), two in India, and one in Mexico. All these nestings involve the olive ridley, the Kemp's ridley having been exploited so intensively that its arribadas have been reduced to fewer than 250 turtles at a time. The evolutionary strategy of mass nesting seems to be one of overwhelming predators through the sheer number of turtles coming ashore.

The largest arribadas in Costa Rica take place usually every month between August and November. Their timing is even fairly predictable, according to Stephen Cornelius, a biologist with the World Wildlife Fund who has studied the turtles of Ostional and Nancite. "The record shows that the majority of arribadas at Nancite occur during the third-quarter moon," he told me. "At Ostional many also occur during the first quarter. During both moon phases the tide is coming in at dusk, but the third-quarter moon offers an added advantage by not rising until nearly midnight—perhaps making it a more attractive time to initiate an arribada, since the first four to six hours after sunset are dark."

Once nesting begins, the turtles are locked into what is called a behavioral groove. You can shine lights in their eyes, drum on their shells, steal their eggs as they're being laid, and still nothing will impede their biological imperative. At night I would sit on washed-up logs and observe the slow-motion surge around me. Turtles are beautiful swimmers, their long front flippers propelling them with rapid grace. On land they look tortured as they drag what has suddenly become a millstone of a body inch by plodding inch over the beach. They wheeze, and syrupy tears drip down their scaly primordial faces as salt is purged from their systems. Their shells—the marvelous protective architecture that has enabled turtles to survive almost unchanged for 150 million years—often show evidence of shark attacks or collisions with boats.

Once an olive ridley, the smallest of the sea turtles, reaches land, the entire nesting process requires about 45 minutes. As soft eggs the size of Ping-Pong balls drop into the hole, the female turtle shuts her eyes and seems to fall into a trance. Then, after deftly refilling the nest, tamping it firm with a side-to-side rocking of her body, and camouflaging it with swipes of her flippers, the turtle drags herself back to her buoyant home without even a parting glance.

Of the 17 million eggs deposited on Playa Ostional, only about 1,428,000 (8.4 percent) were destined to hatch. Fungi, parasites, high temperatures, and other factors would prevent more than two-thirds from hatching or even developing. At least one in six eggs would be destroyed by turtles digging up one another's nests. Predators such as ghost crabs, dogs, and pigs might also take a heavy toll. But the greatest egg predators invariably are humans. During the October 1989 arribada, they extracted more than three-quarters of a million eggs.

Unfortunately for the sea turtles of Costa Rica, their eggs are avidly sought after as aphrodisiacs. Turtle eggs, sand still clinging to them, are sold in many of the country's bars, where the yolk is mixed with hot sauce and downed in a shot glass. The traditional association of turtle eggs with libido perhaps comes from the proclivity of sea turtles to engage in hours-long couplings.

When I first arrived at Playa Ostional, the beach was dotted with *hueveros*—egg collectors. They were digging up fresh nests with their hands, scooping out eggs, and dropping them into large bags. Mario Alvarado, a young biologist hired by the village association, saw me glaring at a pack of hueveros and reminded me that egg harvesting was legal at certain times on Playa Ostional. Turtle eggs, he said, have long been the cash crop of these coastal villagers.

I knew Mario from just having driven six hours with him from the capital city of San José. To me he is an unsung hero of the fledgling conservation movement in Central America. With the help of Stephen Cornelius, he has devised an innovative management plan for Ostional, a plan that is successfully balancing the traditional needs of the villagers with the mandate of protecting an endangered turtle species. Under a law enacted in the 1980s, local residents can collect eggs during the first 36 hours of an arribada, supervised by guards supplied by the association. After that, armed guards are assigned at night to protect the nests from poachers. The women of the village are asked to collect any newborn turtles that emerge in the perilous dawn hours and carry them safely to the sea.

That was a satisfying sight—women and children carrying bucketfuls of newly hatched turtles down to the water's edge. It was a happy coincidence that eggs laid during an arribada nearly two months before were hatching at the same time another nesting frenzy was occurring. Even as adult turtles were dragging themselves up the beach, two-inch-long hatchlings were breaking through the sand and instinctively heading toward the ocean.

Seeing gangs of black vultures poised to pick off the baby turtles, I began rescuing them myself. Holding a perfectly formed baby turtle in my palm, I could feel the strength of its swimming motion as it flailed its tiny forelimbs in the air. I turned toward the growing light over the water and with pleasure dropped the little turtle into the Pacific Ocean, away from us alien land beings.

Reptiles and amphibians in general lead secretive and solitary lives. Still, it came as a surprise that sometimes I could walk at night in a tropical forest and not hear a single frog calling or within the arc of my flashlight not see a single salamander, lizard, or snake. I had assumed that these moisture-loving, heat-craving creatures would be as common a sight in the humid forests as stoop sitters are on a summer evening in a big city. But although the diversity of amphibians and reptiles is high in the tropics, the number of individuals in each species is low, and each one has its preferred microhabitat. Most of these creatures are difficult to spot anyway, garbed as they are in the protective camouflage of colors of the forest. *(Continued on page 92)*

Leaving their watery home, olive ridley sea turtles arrive en masse to lay eggs on Playa Ostional along Costa Rica's Pacific coast. An estimated 180,000 female turtles came ashore during this five-day **arribada**, or mass nesting emergence. Each turtle spends about 45 minutes on land, time enough to deposit eggs and cover them with sand. Opposite, village children collect the eggs of an ailing ridley that spilled its clutch on the protected beach.
BILL CURTSINGER (BOTH)

Digging frantically, olive ridley hatchlings extricate themselves from a nest. Where baby ridleys, like the one below, go once they reach the open sea remains a mystery. Opposite, one of many poachers takes the eggs of a leatherback nesting on Playa Grande in Costa Rica.

BILL CURTSINGER (ALL)

Rare daytime nesting of a leatherback, largest of the marine turtles, prompts a Scout patrol on Playa Tamarindo in Costa Rica to cool off the giant reptile. The Scouts help guard the beach against poachers. Its duty done, a leatherback (above) laboriously heads seaward.

Thrill-seeking visitors are often acutely disappointed if they don't stumble upon a snake—the bigger the better; never mind that the limbless reptile might be a fer-de-lance, bushmaster, tropical rattlesnake, or eyelash viper, to name but a few of the dangerous pit vipers of the American tropics. According to seasoned herpetologists, the chances of encountering a venomous snake in the rain forest are slim. During my two months in the tropical wilds I never saw a dangerous serpent, though I heard enough eyewitness accounts of huge bushmasters— among the most venomous snakes in the New World—to convince me not to daydream during forest walks.

The bushmaster has perfected the nocturnal ambush. Its long, forked tongue, flicking in the air, can pick up chemical clues to the whereabouts of nearby prey. Say it "tastes" a mouse in the vicinity. Closing in on its invisible prey, the bushmaster now employs its special heat-sensing organ. All pit vipers have a depression, or pit, on each side of the head between the eye and nostril. The membrane in the pit is extremely sensitive to changes in temperature, and it detects infrared heat rays. The bushmaster now locates its target, measuring the precise direction of any warm-blooded being that differs in temperature from the general background. In total darkness the bushmaster coils and strikes, burying its long fangs in the unsuspecting prey, paralyzing it with an injection of poison.

There are two things to remember when you're looking for amphibians and reptiles in the rain forest, says herpetologist Douglas Robinson: Never stand still without first checking the ground around you for snakes and army ants; and don't point your hands—you'll frighten animals away. With these principles in mind, I went on a specimen-gathering expedition with Douglas, an American scientist who has taught in the University of Costa Rica's biology department for more than 20 years. We were joined by one of his students, Eberhard Meyer from West Germany.

The three of us focused our attention on the Península de Osa, an area of pristine lowland forest in southernmost Costa Rica near the Panama border, on the Pacific Ocean side. Teacher and student didn't have to reach the wilderness to begin collecting, however. We pulled off the highway in a mountain pass to look under rocks for salamanders. We stopped at a hillside stream where women were washing clothes and plunged into the foliage to hunt for frogs. In the truck-stop town of Palmar Norte one night, Eberhard donned waders and a headlamp and sloshed through roadside ditches to search for amphibians. Another time we followed the siren calls of frogs into a cacao plantation.

"You never know where you might find something down here," Douglas said. "Once I was holed up with my students in a hotel in the town of Golfito during a downpour. A cleaning woman was sweeping the ceiling of the dining room with a long-handled broom, and she knocked a gecko down from the rafters. It turned out to be a new species for Costa Rica."

Reaching the swamps and forest of the peninsula, we reverted to our normal diurnal habits. Our mission was to catch poison-dart frogs, multihued amphibians of the dendrobatid family. Some species produce toxins so poisonous that Indians in the rain forest of Colombia hunt game with blowgun darts smeared with the venomous mucus. Dendrobatids, unlike most tropical frogs, feed and breed during daylight hours, when their warning coloration can be readily seen.

I learned firsthand about frog toxins when I snatched up a fleshy tropical bullfrog from a culvert in Palmar Norte. I had a paper cut on the base of a thumb, and for a few minutes after holding the large frog my hand went tingly, then numb; the skin toxin had entered my bloodstream. All amphibians secrete toxins, most of them not very potent. The skin secretions of certain types of frogs and toads, however, amount to biological warfare. Hypertension, vasoconstriction, convulsions, cardiac arrest, respiratory paralysis, and hallucinations are among the symptoms caused by the most powerful of these toxins. A key ingredient inducing the trancelike state of zombies in voodoo ritual is toxin taken from huge marine toads, nuisance animals that collect in large numbers in many Central American villages. From certain brightly colored dendrobatids scientists have extracted the most poisonous substances known in nature.

Into the forest Douglas, Eberhard, and I went, perspiring heavily in the humid gloom, cupping our hands around our ears to distinguish the telltale chirping of our quarry. The dendrobatids we caught (I cleaned my hands after each encounter) were truly spectacular. *Dendrobates auratus* has a neon green body spotted in black. *Phyllobates vittatus*, one of the most poisonous frogs, appears in Halloween colors of black and orange. *Dendrobates granuliferus* is called the strawberry frog for the granular red coloring of its back; its legs are blue-green.

The strawberry frogs seemed particularly brazen, shunning shadows, perching on the high buttress roots of trees, calling loudly for mates. No amphibian furtiveness here.

"They want to be seen," said Eberhard. Color-perceiving predators such as birds and lizards are meant to take notice and think twice before attacking. "The poisons are probably not intended to kill anything," Eberhard added. "They are supposed to make the frog taste bad. If you kill a predator, you haven't taught it a lesson."

I remember thinking at the time of all the frogs and turtles I had seen in the tropics, and all the snakes I hadn't seen but had definitely imagined, and realizing that life in the wild could be viewed as terrifyingly basic. Hunt and be hunted. If you are small, don't expect to live long. Find a mate and breed. Forage and reproduce.

Perhaps sensing my mood, Eberhard nodded toward the underbrush where one strawberry frog appeared to be approaching another on the prop roots of a tall tree. "A male and female," he whispered. "I think that when they are breeding these frogs are very tender, just by the way I have seen them touch each other." Yes, it did lift my spirits to think that maybe the pleasure principle did operate after all in a snake-eat-frog world.

I resumed my nocturnal pursuits when I returned in the dry season to Guyana to look for black caimans, largest of the New World crocodilians. The black caiman, which in general form closely resembles the American alligator, grows as long as 20 feet, though such giants are becoming exceedingly rare. Once abundant throughout the Amazon basin, the black caiman has suffered terribly at the hands of hide hunters since the 1930s, to the point that its population is estimated to have fallen to only a few thousand—perhaps less than one percent of its 19th-century numbers. To observe this endangered species, I ventured one February into Guyana's remote Rupununi savannas, near the Brazilian border, where one of the last strongholds of the black caiman survives.

The broad, slow Rupununi River winds through the extensive tropical grasslands of southwestern Guyana. Small, widely scattered Indian villages sit on its jungly banks. Herons stand sentinel every mile or so in the riverine vegetation. In the dry season the falling river exposes steep sand banks pocked by kingfisher nests. On the periodic sand flats appear nesting tracks of the *tracajá*, a river turtle, and here and there its giant relative, the *arrau*, which grows to weigh more than a hundred pounds, has its nesting grounds. Iguanas bask in the fierce sunlight. Downpours come and go.

Beneath the calm surface of the Rupununi swims a host of formidable creatures. There are electric eels, piranhas, stingrays, anacondas—the largest of the boas—and, most fearsome of all, the *candirú*, a needle-thin catfish that is known to enter the human urethral opening and implant itself with sharp spines.

All scatter at the approach of a black caiman, the powerful, massively armored crocodilian that is South America's largest predator. During the day I would see a few lurking beneath the tangled vegetation at the river's edge, their knobbed eyes and broad snouts visible at the water's surface, their bull necks layered with dark scales that have been described as being as thick and tough as the heel of a boot. Swift and silent hunters, adult black caimans think big when hungry; besides fish, they prey on young cattle, wading birds, capybaras, small deer, pigs, and other caimans. Black caimans may also attack humans, though such behavior is rare. At Apoteri village I saw an Indian boy who had lost an arm to a caiman while fishing, and at Yupukari I heard how a caiman had lashed a canoe with its tail, toppling a village boy into the water—and into the reptile's gaping jaws.

Black caimans of course are no match for humans with guns. The caimans are prime targets because their large, relatively smooth belly skins are a prized, though illegal, commodity in the leather business.

Fishermen also kill caimans because they think the carnivorous reptiles interfere with their catch. Evidence suggests, however, that when the caiman population drops, fish stocks may decline as well. Nutrients from the black caiman's excrement are thought to form the base of some aquatic food chains.

After four days of river travel I stopped at Karanambo, a Texas-scale cattle ranch run by Diane McTurk. Tall and thin as a stilt, Diane usually greets her guests in the company of two unusual pets—a silky, five-foot-long giant otter that swims with her in the Rupununi, and a chunky, two-foot-high capybara, a giant rodent with webbed hind toes that looks like a cross between a beaver and a pig. Having quit a public relations job in England to move to Guyana in 1977, Diane has watched wildlife populations there decline precipitously. "The human population in the savanna has gone up and the animal ones have gone down," she said in a refined English accent. "Everyone is hunting." A convert to conservation, one of the few in her country, Diane is lobbying the Guyanese government to designate a 250-square-mile section of the savanna as a wildlife reserve. Meanwhile, she often hears gunshots on the river at night as hunters blast the big caimans.

Well-disguised by day, caimans become easy targets at night. Their eyes, reflecting the beam of a flashlight, glow like cigarette embers. Pairs of red eyes gleam along the banks, in the flooded thickets, gliding rapidly across the breadth of the river.

One cloudy, buggy evening, out in a small motor launch, I counted ten of the big reptiles in a half-mile stretch of river—both black caimans and the smaller common caimans. The crocodilians allowed the boat to drift as close as a few feet, near enough for me to discern the long, thickly scaled bodies floating at 45-degree angles in the water.

The presence of caimans on the river electrified the wilderness for me. I was sharing space with a living relative of the dinosaurs, man and beast alert to one another, each capable of taking the life of the other. That night our river party made camp on a sliver of sand backed by flooded forest. Before I climbed into my hammock, I cast my light a last time over the water. Five pairs of red eyes gleamed nearby.

Loud splashes sounded throughout the night as fish jumped and caimans hunted. Heavy rain descended, and the river began to rise, inching toward our low-slung hammocks. Caimans swam menacingly into my dreams; mine was not an easy sleep. Yet in a strange way the power of the caimans to frighten felt cleansing to me. It restored in my mind a sense of an ancient wilderness balance between the hunter and the hunted, one in which man had more to fear than the caiman did— a balance that allowed the night to protect its own. □

During the dry season sideneck turtles mob together in a
lagoon on the Orinoco River floodplain in Venezuela.
Feared by most water creatures, a black caiman (opposite),
largest of the New World crocodilians, lurks in the soupy
waters of a river in Guyana.
BRIAN ROGERS / BIOFOTOS (ABOVE); JANY SAUVANET / PITCH (OPPOSITE)

PAGES 98–99: Clouds of spray rise from mighty
Kaieteur Falls, 822 feet high, in central Guyana.
The swollen waters humidify dense rain forest, haven for
scores of moisture-loving amphibian and reptile species.
BILL CURTSINGER

Ocean Worlds:

Secret Places Undersea

We live on an ocean planet. The sea laps at the shores of the continents, surrounding and defining the land. Viewed from space, the oceans are connected as one, but beneath the surface there are great divides, invisible walls. There are countries of life in the sea. Their boundaries are not rivers and mountain ranges, but currents and differences in water depth and temperature. Bill Curtsinger and I have made many journeys to the countries beneath the oceans. He has dived under the ice at both ends of the globe; seen surface light dappling the back of a walrus in the cold Chukchi Sea; heard humpback whales singing in the dark blue waters around Hawaii. I have watched sharks mating off the tip of the Sinai in the Red Sea; seen green turtles nesting on a sandy islet in the Great Barrier Reef; held out my hand to a sea lion in the waters off South Australia and felt his whiskers tickle my palm. In the pages that follow we present three underwater worlds, visual jewels in the sea: coral reefs off New Guinea, a fjord in New Zealand, and waters around Antarctica, where Bill descended through tide cracks in the ice (opposite) to document life in the depths below. As visitors in the earth's oceans, Bill and I have gone to these hidden places to portray the wonder of their native creatures, eye to eye.

David Doubilet

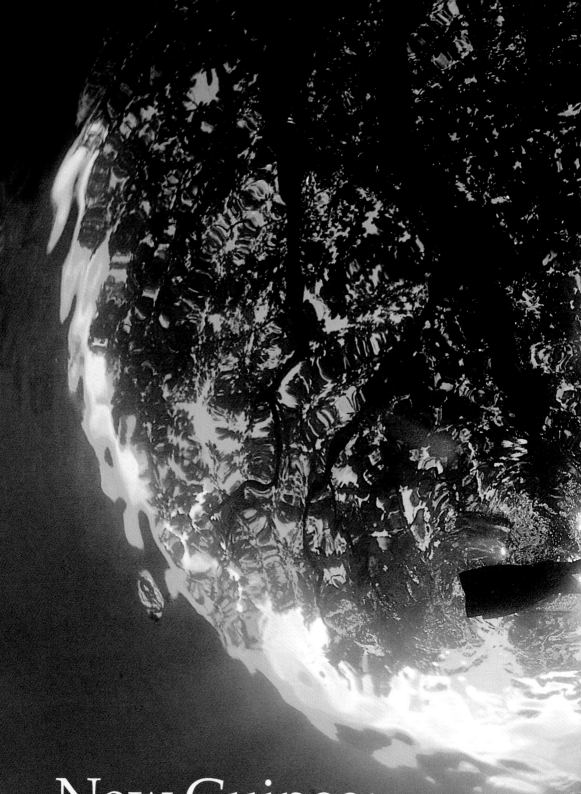

New Guinea:

Marvels of a Coral Reef

Dense rain forest edging the coast shades tropical
waters along the southeastern tip of New Guinea. Here, David
Doubilet spent several weeks aboard a dive boat "tied
up to a jungle in a wild corner of the Pacific," exploring coral
reefs whose inhabitants rarely see humans.

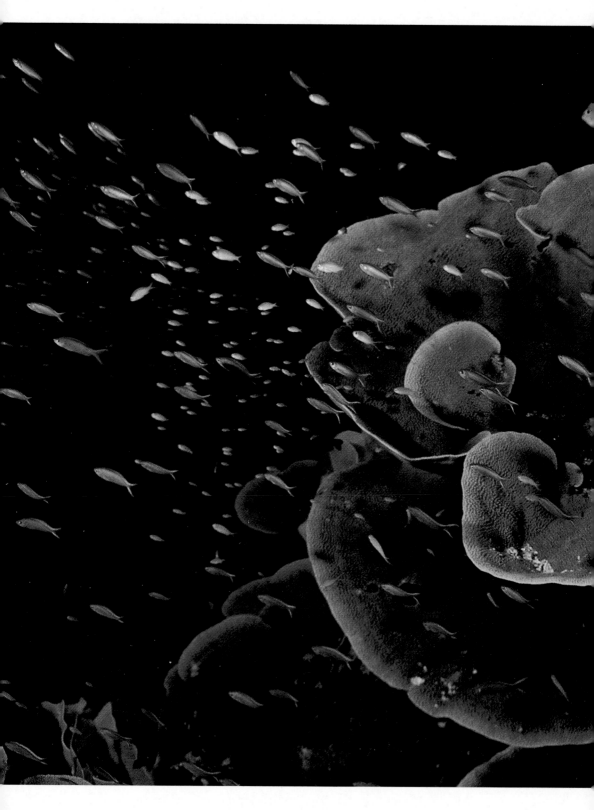

Text and Pictures by
David Doubilet

I t was a simple anchorage. Naturalist Dinah Halstead readied the bow anchor as Bob, her husband, backed the 65-foot dive boat *Telita* into the jungle and tied it to a tree. We were lashed to the side of the huge, brooding island of New Guinea at the edge of the Solomon Sea. The water here is blood-warm, and it cradles one of the richest realms of coral on the planet. Farther out in the Pacific and Indian Oceans the coral reefs are less lush and diverse, with fewer species of fish and invertebrates. Here, I felt I was in the heart of the ocean.

We stepped off the dive platform into a clear-water world of steep, coral-covered cliffs and walls, a world where purple anthiases and yellow damselfish (left) fed on drifting plankton. There is a direct, complex connection between the rain forest and the coral reef. Nutrients from the forest wash into the sea and help feed the phytoplankton, which feed the zooplankton—which feed the coral polyps.

The reef waters around an island like New Guinea, veined as it is with rivers pouring muddy waters into the sea, are usually not very clear. The reefs would be spectacular if you could see them. This end of New Guinea, though, has deep, clear water right up to the forest along the shore, making the reefs below a painterly dream. □

In the shadows of shoreline trees grow
forests of gorgonians, giant corals that
usually thrive 80 feet down, in depths of
perpetual blue twilight. On one I found a
small goby (above) hiding in the branches
like a bird, then looked up through the
coral treetops as an outrigger canoe floated
across a watery sky (opposite).

FOLLOWING PAGES: A few miles offshore, on
a reef now named Doubilet's, Bob Halstead
swam through a living waterfall of silver
baitfish feeding in the pulsing currents.

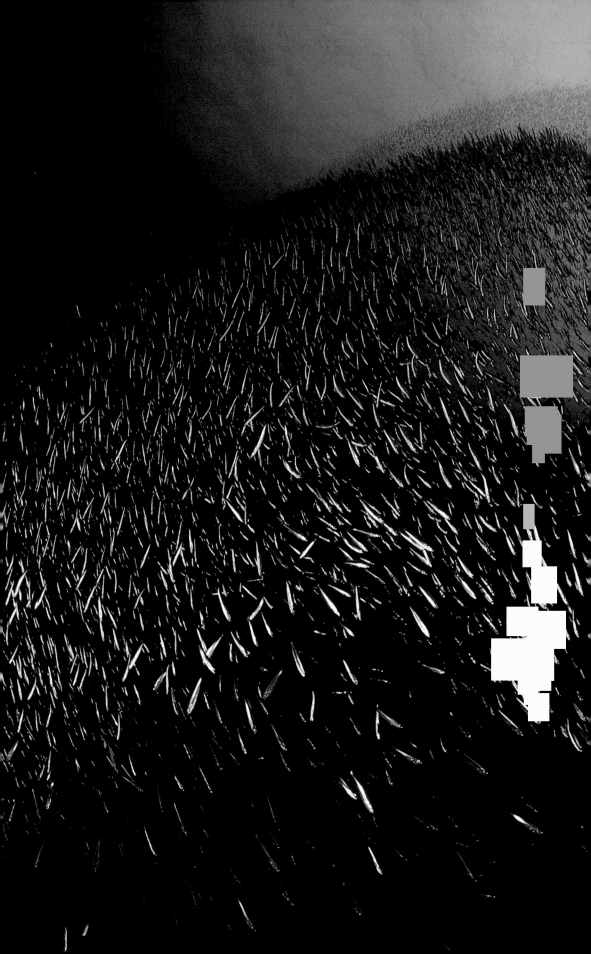

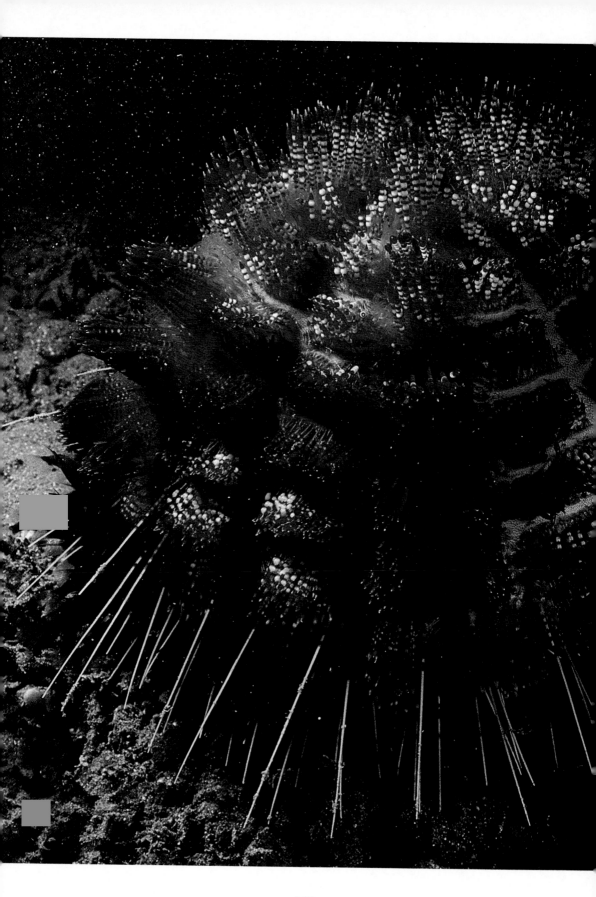

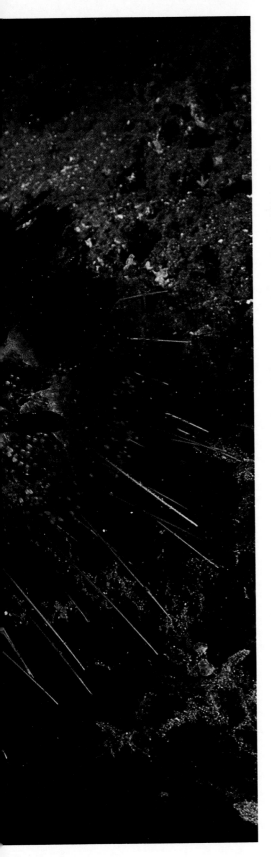

Illuminated by my flash, a fire urchin (left) resembling an alien spacecraft grazes on the black sand bottom 60 feet down. When I approached, it bristled like a psychotic cat. Up close, I found tiny shrimp (above) living safely amid the urchin's venomous spines.

FOLLOWING PAGES: *A pair of clownfish burrow among the purple tentacles of a sea anemone as it closes up for the night.*

New Zealand:

Treasures of a Southern Fjord

*Light of a winter sunset seeps through storm clouds
over Doubtful Sound, a secluded arm of the Tasman Sea along
the west coast of New Zealand's South Island—a region of
dramatic fjords holding unexpected undersea life.
David Doubilet calls it "a secret ocean between the South
Pacific tropics and the howling winds of the polar seas."*

Text and Pictures by
David Doubilet

T he rumble of *Renown*'s diesel broke the silence of Doubtful Sound. The throb of the engine rolled across the calm waters and bounced against steep, forested walls. The surface was completely smooth, mirroring a sky heavy with Tasman Sea clouds streaked with light. A group of dolphins, permanent residents of the sound, joined the research vessel, slipping into position ahead of the bow wave to pursue their favorite sport, submarine surfing. That morning the dolphins (opposite) seemed ghostlike, formed of light and shadow. Then, one by one, they slid off the bow wave and disappeared into the fjord's thousand-foot depths.

The South Island's big fjord systems, called sounds, were carved by glaciers, and Doubtful Sound is by far the most beautiful. From its opening on the edge of the Tasman Sea it stretches far into the interior, and the arm of the sea becomes a multifingered hand reaching into 3,000-foot mountain walls. It can be torn apart instantly by 60-mile-an-hour winds that scream down the cliffs. Storms coming in from the Tasman Sea, storms that formed thousands of miles away over the ocean around Antarctica, make this region one of the wettest on earth. Heavy rains and snows and waterfalls rushing down the fjord walls cover the sea with a layer of fresh water as deep as 25 feet, stained dark with runoff from the land. Just beneath that murky layer are animals normally seen at great depths—tricked by the darkness of the surface layer into living higher up—and cold, clear waters where few humans have ever been.

A thin sheet of ice covered Doubtful Sound the day I dived there with marine biologist Roger Grace and his diving partner, Linda Ingham. The surface layer was one degree above freezing, and it burned the exposed parts of my face between my mask and diving hood. By comparison, the winter sea below the freshwater layer felt warm. Between the two layers is a zone where the lighter fresh water and the heavy ocean water meet and mix. Everything there seemed out of focus. The water looked like crystal smoke. It was for me a hazy doorway into another world, and I descended through it into a cold, still place that was dark and clear—and silent. □

Along a cliff wall 75 feet down, we saw delicate trees of black coral—eerie gray-white in the light of my strobes—with a snake star (below) tightly coiled on one branch. In the open sea such corals would be found at depths of 100 feet or more, but in these dark waters they can live much higher up. As Linda Ingham swam above the coral forest into the green freshwater layer (opposite), her rising bubbles made holes in the surface, creating the effect of an undersea sky full of miniature storm clouds.

Late one afternoon we dived into the emerald sea to a black coral 50 feet down—a giant submarine topiary (below). It had a fuzzy-looking cloud near its midsection, as if it were smoking. Smoking? The coral was spawning, releasing masses of microscopic eggs—and I was witnessing one of the rarest sights in the sea. Nearby, mating nudibranchs were entwined on a piece of coral (right), their carnation colors glorious in the dark green depths.

Hordes of crayfish clung to the ledges of
a wall above the black coral. In the cold water
they were sluggish, waving their antennae
slowly. I examined one—an armored
samurai in full battle dress—covered with
hooks and horns and knobbed protrusions
guarding obsidian eyes (opposite). Then
I shone my light behind a kelp leaf to watch
a sea spider crawl across (above). It was
strange to see this creature move with the
same gait as its land-bound cousins in this
ocean avenue enclosed by high green walls.

Antarctica:

Wonders Under Ice

*A flock of emperor penguins streaks through
polar waters of McMurdo Sound. "They zoomed by
like a squadron of F-16s, undersea aviators
maneuvering through their under-ice domain," says
Bill Curtsinger, who has made five
journeys to Antarctica's frigid waters to
photograph their little-known wildlife
and otherworldly beauty.*

Text and Pictures by
Bill Curtsinger

Sitting at the edge of the dive hole, I look into water so clear that I can spy a white sponge on the bottom a hundred feet down. Once I saw a Weddell seal glide by as I stared into the hole before a dive. Its swimming appeared effortless as it turned and looked up at me. The seal's window, and mine, is a small, round hole cut through eight feet of Antarctic sea ice near the shore of McMurdo Sound. The water temperature is 28°F; the diving is rugged. Unlike the seal, which was born with the proper insulation needed to live here, I am dressed as I must be to survive even a brief dive, enveloped in a "dry suit" of rubber, with several layers of wool and cotton underneath. I feel warm in the heated hut over the dive hole, but that sensation will vanish when I slip down under the ice.

Below me lies a dark, primordial sea full of drifting plankton and primitive-looking organisms. The waters around Antarctica are an isolated environment. Frigid currents circling the continent form a temperature barrier that prevents temperate-water creatures from floating in and surviving here. During the Antarctic summer the sun shines constantly, and masses of plankton bloom in the water. By the end of the season the plankton that make Antarctica's seas among the most productive on earth also make the water so cloudy that you can't see your hand in front of your face. But in the spring, when I have come here, the water is gin clear; visibility distances that divers normally measure in tens of feet can be measured in hundreds.

Under the ice the black waters sparkle with tiny zooplankton. Jellyfish, some larger than a diver, prey on small creatures borne on the currents. Looking up, I see long, jagged tide cracks in the black ceiling of snow-covered ice above me. At the surface they appear uninteresting, but down here they look like bolts of white lightning streaking across a night sky. Weddell seals ascend the tide cracks to breathe (opposite) and often surface within our dive hut, sometimes with freshly caught fish. Underwater the seals make eerie trilling sounds, and they swim with a mesmerizing serpentine motion. Theirs is part of the rarely seen beauty that lures me into these waters. □

*In the flash of my camera strobe, jellyfish—
including the common helmet (top) and
Diplulumaris antarctica (above)—glow like
stars in the dimly lit waters. Anemones and soft
corals cover a ridge (opposite).*

*FOLLOWING PAGES: Red starfish, the seafloor's
top predators, feed on a sponge near a marine
worm. Down here I feel like a voyager in true inner
space, sweeping my underwater light, looking for
a twinkle in the darkness.*

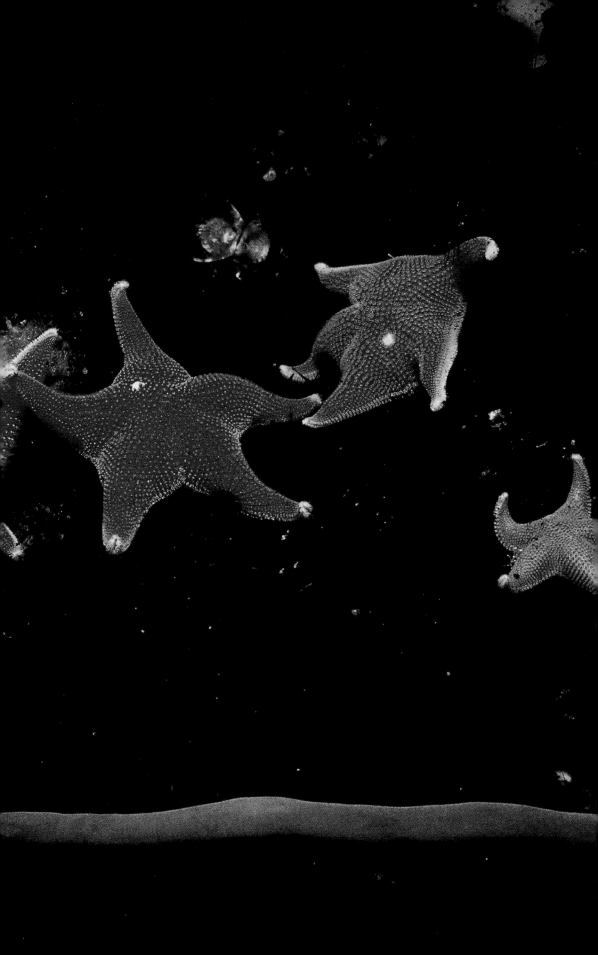

Kluane:

A Yukon Wilderness

Squaring off in an annual autumn rite, Dall rams repeatedly rear up, race toward each other, and butt heads to gain dominance. This pair battles atop Sheep Mountain in Kluane National Park Reserve, a vast, rugged wilderness covering 8,500 square miles in the southwestern corner of Canada's Yukon Territory.

FRANK OBERLE

Text by Kim Heacox

Photographs by Stephen J. Krasemann

There's a land where the mountains are nameless,
And the rivers all run God knows where;
There are lives that are erring and aimless,
And deaths that just hang by a hair;
There are hardships that nobody reckons;
There are valleys unpeopled and still;
There's a land—oh, it beckons and beckons,
And I want to go back—and I will.

I t was nearly 90 years ago that Robert W. Service penned those lines, in a poem about Canada's northwesternmost territory. "The Spell of the Yukon," he called it. Gold had been discovered on the Klondike, a tributary of the mighty Yukon River, and prospectors had arrived like locusts to seek their fortunes. The towns of Dawson and Whitehorse had sprung up as fast as fireweed, and legends had spread about bears and wolves and the men who had fought them. This was the land of Jack London's *Call of the Wild* and *White Fang*, of Service's "Cremation of Sam McGee" and "The Shooting of Dan McGrew." Fiction, yes, but inspired by fact, for the words speak of landscape, wildlife, and survival—the spirit of the Yukon.

That same spirit lives on today, and nowhere more strongly than down in the Yukon Territory's southwest corner by the big lake called Kluane (Kloo-AHN-ee). Here the land runs to the east in meadows and bluffs and forests of aspen and spruce, while to the west the lofty St. Elias Mountains rise without preamble to catch storms blowing in from the Gulf of Alaska. Snow falls every month of the year in those rocky ramparts, creating the largest subpolar ice-field system outside Greenland. In all of North America a more inhospitable place can hardly be found. Here the Ice Age has not ended, but merely retreated. From these ice fields flow more than 2,000 glaciers—great rivers of ice patterned by crevasses and moraines, grinding rock into sediment, descending valleys, and eventually melting into braided rivers with names such as Alsek, Donjek, Dusty, Kaskawulsh, and Slims.

At roughly latitude 60° north—twice as close to the North Pole as to the Equator—the Kluane wilderness is largely locked in the grip of winter. Even in the interior lowlands east of the mountains, the weather is often bitterly cold and capricious. The wind comes up suddenly, the usual way, and whitecaps churn the lakes. The sky grows sullen, the mercury drops. The night wind's howls are broken now and then by other howling, that of wolves. But perhaps the next morning sunlight will melt the air, thrushes and robins will sing, and a bull moose will chew willow right outside your tent. You'll catch his eye as he catches yours, one mammal assessing another in a transcendental moment, and the moose will pause, shake his head, and resume feeding.

"The great hurrah about wild animals is that they exist at all," wrote Annie Dillard in *Pilgrim at Tinker Creek*, "and the greater hurrah is the actual moment of seeing them." Hundreds of those moments exist in Kluane country, but only if you slow down and read the land carefully. A lynx might appear in a clearing, a mountain goat on a ridge, a bear along a river. Few places in North America have a greater diversity of wild animals—or a greater ability to hide them.

Here the subarctic climate meets the temperate, the mountains meet the plains, taiga meets tundra, and a rich montage of habitats results. More than 45 species of mammals and well over 100 bird species can be found in this wild corner of the Yukon. Wolves and coyotes, grizzly bears and black bears, mountain goats and Dall sheep, lynxes and hares, owls and eagles, predators and prey, migrators and hibernators, nocturnal and diurnal creatures—they're all here. Surely if Noah ever dropped anchor in northern North America, Kluane was the place.

I n 1942 the Alaska Highway was completed from Dawson Creek, British Columbia, to Fairbanks, Alaska, slicing through the southwest corner of the Yukon Territory, skirting Kluane Lake and fronting the St. Elias Mountains. Concern for wildlife prompted the territorial government to establish the Kluane Game Sanctuary in 1943. But many considered the protection insufficient, and after decades of debate and compromise Kluane National Park was established in 1972. (The designation "Reserve" was added four years later.) Covering 8,500 square miles—an area more than half the size of Switzerland—Kluane National Park Reserve is among the largest and youngest of Canada's wilderness parklands. A further distinction came in 1979 when Kluane and its Alaska neighbor, Wrangell–St. Elias National Park and Preserve, were recognized by the United Nations Educational, Scientific and Cultural Organization (UNESCO) as a joint World Heritage Site.

I first experienced Kluane many years ago, and though mine was a short visit, only half a day, the memories crystallized within me like hoarfrost. It was early March and minus 20 degrees Fahrenheit outside, typical weather for Kluane at that time of year. Heading north on the Alaska Highway, I had wool clothing, *(Continued on page 142)*

"Like gunshots going off," says photographer Frank
Oberle of the collisions as rams meet head-to-head (above)
during the November–December rut. After more than
an hour of charging and butting, the loser walked away head
down, leaving the victor (opposite) battered but unbowed—
and ready to mate with ewes to sire another generation.
FRANK OBERLE (BOTH)

*Startling in winter white, an ermine (left) pops up
from the underbrush to survey its still snowless realm.
Agile and quick, ermines are relentless hunters, often
preying on mice in grassy or boggy areas like this
one around a beaver pond near the Auriol Range (above).*
FRANK OBERLE (LEFT)

*FOLLOWING PAGES: Resplendent in sweeping antlers,
a woodland caribou grazes low-growing alpine tundra
vegetation in the Burwash Uplands near Kluane.*

a sleeping bag, and chocolates stashed in my car in case of an emergency. The air was cold enough to make your teeth ache. Water froze instantly, oil turned to glop, even the air had a strange viscosity. Ice and snow patterned the ground in ridges and drifts, while the distant mountains glistened like wolf fangs against a cloudless, lapis lazuli sky.

After crossing the Slims River where it flows into Kluane Lake, I pulled off the road and stepped out into the subarctic air. A dozen pairs of eyes were on me, each framed by white hair and curling horns. The animals watching me so intently were Dall sheep, the world's only species of wild white sheep. I took out my binoculars to watch them. They stood on a slope only a few hundred feet above, all rams, motionless, their breath forming crystals in the air. Then they began to move slowly across the slope. For reasons I still can't explain and have never regretted, I trudged up and waited in the path of the rams. Ice caked my moustache, the cold numbed my fingers. It wouldn't be long before the chill wind would force me back down to my car. Yet that same wind had exposed the meager plant life on which the sheep grazed, moving slowly and looking up now and then at the six-foot biped ahead. One hundred feet away, fifty, thirty — they came straight toward me. I sat down in an effort to appear nonthreatening.

Clearly visible were the annual growth rings on the rams' horns. Unlike male members of the deer family, which shed their antlers every autumn and grow new ones the following spring and summer, male sheep grow a single set of horns and retain them for life. Each year another ring is added. Count the rings, like those of a tree, and you have the age of the ram. As near as I could tell, some of the rams approaching me were ten years old or more, their horns in full, sweeping curves.

Twenty feet away and they stopped, their eyes suspicious, curious. They lowered their heads, and I realized that any one of them could charge and perhaps kill me. But they moved on, grazing as they passed by and disappeared over the ridge. And for a moment, sitting on that frozen ground as the magical encounter came and went, I forgot about the cold. I drove away that day half astonished at myself and half astonished at the sheep. No sooner had I left the Yukon than it began to beckon, as Robert Service said it would, and I kept thinking about the Dall sheep out there in the cold, living and dying, adding drama to an already dramatic land. The park called Kluane had put its spell on me.

Many times since then I have driven the Alaska Highway south from my home in Anchorage, and every time I have been in too great a hurry to stop and visit Kluane. Schedules and deadlines have too often controlled my life, but that changed one recent September when my wife, Melanie, and I made a trip to Kluane. An autumn palette colored the land — yellow aspens, orange birches, green spruces, red tundra, and a dusting of snow on the mountaintops. As we drove south past Kluane Lake, bound for the town of Haines Junction, it was twilight, and up ahead a coyote crossed the road. Or was it a wolf? We pulled over and peered into the dwarf birch where the animal had crossed, but saw nothing. In five seconds whatever it was had disappeared.

"Sounds like a coyote to me," an old man told us in Burwash Landing, on the northwestern shore of the lake. "But ya know," he added, "there was a couple packs of wolves got to howlin' back and forth across the lake here last winter. Come mornin' you'd see their tracks around the place. Some folks said they could tell the packs apart from the sounds they made. I swear it went on for hours some nights, all that howlin'. It kinda sent a chill up yer spine."

Ron Chambers has lived in this country all his life. His mother, now in her seventies, still runs a trapline on the east side of Kluane Lake. Ron is half Tlingit, the native blood of southeast Alaska. When Kluane National Park Reserve was established, many locals protested, complaining that new regulations would disrupt their traditional ways. But Ron heard a different drummer and became a park warden. He has camped on glaciers, run wild rivers, and climbed imposing mountains, including Mount Logan, the highest peak in Canada. In a grandiose, northwestern way, Kluane is Ron's Walden Pond. He has experienced all its seasons and moods, and wouldn't want to live anywhere else.

When I asked Ron what animal best embodies the spirit of Kluane, I expected him to choose the grizzly or moose or wolf, something powerful and unpredictable, like the land itself. He leaned back for a moment, deliberateness being a trademark of folks in the Yukon, and smiled and said, "The wolf, yes—he's a powerful survivor. But also the raven. Drive along the highway here for as many years as I have, and you'll see road-killed hawks, owls, jays, hares, coyotes, moose, and others, but never ravens. They're very intelligent, and that's just as important as strength to survive here."

In Tlingit legend, the Great Raven controlled the sun, moon, and stars; his grandson, Trickster Raven, stole them all, made the earth from mud and rocks, and set out on a series of comical adventures. The roots of Tlingit humor—and lively humor it is—can be found in the tales of ravens. One contemporary story, reportedly true, tells of a raven that lands just beyond the reach of a chained dog. The dog, as slow-witted as the raven is smart, wakes up, runs full speed at the black bird, reaches the end of its chain, and crumples to the ground. The raven, having nonchalantly held its position the entire time, and now only two feet from the panting dog, squawks indignantly and flies away.

Ron explained that it's not just along the highway that ravens excel. Go into the heart of the park where you'll see nothing but ice, rock, and snow. Listen. The wind howls, an avalanche rumbles, your heart pounds. A sea of ice extends in all directions, broken on the horizon by lofty, rocky summits. Two-thirds of Kluane National Park Reserve looks like this. Save for you and your companions, there is no sign of life. Not immediately, anyway. Then two ravens soar into view, mates for life. They pass overhead, do full barrel rolls, and fly on. It's food that brings them to the ice fields, however, not antics. Westerly storms off the Gulf of Alaska blow small birds inland from the coast, especially during spring and fall migrations. Even geese and swans lose their way. Once stranded, they become cold, disoriented, incapable of flying out. The ravens descend and make a meal of them.

As harsh as it is, and as lifeless as it appears, the icy realm of Kluane holds pleasant surprises. Some small birds do in fact live here—snow buntings, rosy finches, and water pipits, for example. They have adapted to survive where others cannot. If you spend enough time on the glaciers, you'll see them. A flock might fly right into your camp looking for scraps. The birds feed on seeds, spores, insects—and ice worms.

When first reported more than a century ago, ice worms were considered a joke, and frequently still are. Some people regard them with about as much seriousness as they do Bigfoot. Even the bard of the Yukon, Robert Service, couldn't resist recording the fun when a bunch of saloon rowdies took "a stick of stained spaghetti with two red ink spots for eyes," dropped it in whiskey behind the back of "the gallant Major Brown," told him it was an ice worm, and dared him to drink:

> *He choked . . . he gulped. . . . Thank God! at last*
> *he'd got the horror down.*
> *Then from the crowd went up a roar: "Hooray for*
> *Sourdough Brown!"*
> *With shouts they raised him shoulder high, and gave*
> *a rousing cheer,*
> *But though they praised him to the sky the Major*
> *did not hear.*

The mere thought of what he had done made the gallant major sick to his stomach, and he bolted out the door. The perpetrators of that prank probably never believed ice worms existed, so the joke is partly on them, for ice worms are every bit as real as spaghetti. In 1891 Dr. Israel Russell of the U.S. Geological Survey traveled the Malaspina Glacier, near Kluane, and reported, "In the early morning before the sunlight touched the snow its surface was literally covered with small, slim black worms, about an inch long, and having a remarkable snakelike appearance. These creatures were wiggling over the snow in thousands, but as soon as the sun rose and made its warmth felt, they disappeared beneath the surface." I have seen such worms wiggling over the ice in the Fairweather Range in southeast Alaska. A kind of earthworm, they probably survive by eating red algae that grow on the surfaces of snowfields and glaciers.

Several summers ago Ron Chambers was similarly surprised when he discovered an isolated colony of pikas, small, grayish brown relatives of rabbits and hares, scampering about the slopes of an alpine ridge off Mount Logan. "It was a world unto itself," he told me, "like an island in a sea of ice. And here were these pikas. I couldn't believe it. How they survived there is beyond me. And you wonder how long

144

pikas have been living there. Maybe centuries. Maybe many thousands of years. Maybe they're a separate species or subspecies. This sort of thing really intrigues me."

Intriguing, too, is the fact that pikas don't hibernate. In the course of a fleeting summer they gather quantities of grasses, herbs, and twigs and pile them into haystacks in deep, rocky crevices. Then for eight cold, dark months they live beneath the snow, feeding on the dried plants, and finally emerging when the warm sun returns.

Dall sheep are just as surprising. Northwest of Mount Logan a nunatak—a mountain peak surrounded by glacial ice—runs across the boundary between Kluane and Wrangell–St. Elias national parks. Two glaciers, the Logan and the Walsh, have created this island in a sea of ice. It seems as though it were from another time—a Pleistocene place that drifted and came to rest amid the glaciers of the St. Elias Mountains. And it abounds with some of the largest, handsomest Dall sheep in North America.

Not many people know about this place, but poachers do. In bush planes equipped with tundra tires or skis, they fly in, land, and illegally hunt for sheep. Park rangers and wardens stake out areas in hope of catching them. Some they do, some they don't. "These are relatively young parks," Ron Chambers said. "People used to do whatever they wanted around here. Now they can't. Times are changing, and that irritates them. You might think a park like this is rugged enough to protect itself, and in many ways it is, but not entirely. It's a never ending battle to protect the wildlife here, but I think we're winning."

"The fear of bears is a wonderful thing," a friend once told me. I chewed on this awhile, then let it go. But his words came back to me as I stood with Melanie beside a creek near the Alsek River, staring at a single bear track in the mud. Something moved in the brush nearby. We looked around. There were no trees to climb, no places to hide. Then a noisy magpie popped out of the brush and flew away.

"Seen any grizzlies?" people had asked all week. "Watch out for bears," they had warned us.

The preoccupation with *Ursus arctos horribilis*, the grizzly bear, is everywhere in Kluane, at least in spring and summer, when the bears are out; and no wonder, for perhaps as many as 200 live here. You might see one your first day in the park, or you might stay for weeks and see none. No animal has engendered more myth, fear, and respect than has the grizzly, a living symbol of the North American wilderness. "Griz," we call him; even the name has an edge. He's bigger and stronger than we are, and an easy target for an itchy trigger finger. Lose him, though, and we lose part of ourselves and the place we came from.

Locals had told us a miner had recently shot and wounded a big, old male bear down by Dalton Post just outside the southern end of the park, and we'd better be careful. *(Continued on page 152)*

Born to hoard, a red squirrel survives Kluane's long winters by storing large amounts of food—principally seeds from spruce cones. Some summers it sets aside more than a year's supply. Solitary and highly territorial, the squirrel scolds animals both large and small that dare to venture into its private domain.

Lowbush cranberries amid lichens and dwarf birches (left) offer a nutritious feast, especially for birds and red squirrels. Above, a collared pika, tiny member of the rabbit family, stands guard on a rocky slope. At the first sign of danger, it gives a shrill warning bark, then dashes for cover.

Most formidable of North American mammals, the grizzly ranges widely over the open tundra. With powerful clawed forepaws, this 300-pound female has rolled back turf to scoop out a ground squirrel. Despite their slow, almost clumsy gait, grizzlies can lope through dense underbrush at 30 miles an hour. True omnivores, they feed on roots, berries, sprouts, insects, fish, mammals of all sizes, even carrion. Perhaps 200 roam the park's backcountry.

"They get nasty," a woman had said. Melanie and I had hiked several trails in the park and had seen no sign of bears, until now. And there it was, a single track, perhaps days old, perhaps minutes.

I was reminded of a passage written nearly 30 years ago by naturalist Adolph Murie, who spent 25 summers in Alaska's Mount McKinley National Park (now Denali National Park and Preserve). "I recall the first bear track I ever saw," Murie wrote. "It was my initial day afield in McKinley Park and my brother and I were crossing from Jenny Creek over a rise to Savage River, on our way to the head of the river. One lone track in a patch of mud is all we saw. But the track was a symbol, and more poetic than seeing the bear himself—a delicate and profound approach to the spirit of the Alaska Wilderness. A bear track at any time may create a stronger emotion than the old bear himself, for the imagination is brought into play. You examine the landscape sharply, expecting a bear on every slope as your quickened interest becomes eager and enterprising. The bear is somewhere, and may be anywhere. The country has come alive with a new, rich quality."

Comparisons between Kluane and Denali are irresistible. Both have towering mountains: Kluane with 19,524-foot Mount Logan, the highest peak in Canada, and Denali with 20,320-foot Mount McKinley, the highest in North America. And surrounding each is a penumbra of lesser known yet spectacular peaks, a mountaineers' mecca. Both parks have landscapes of ice, rock, rivers, tundra, and taiga that poets and propagandists have again and again tried, and mostly failed, to describe. And both have a rich panoply of wildlife. But here some differences emerge. In Denali you readily see the wildlife; in Kluane you don't, largely because visitors in Denali travel an unpaved road 85 miles into the park, while those in Kluane only skirt its eastern edge. No road penetrates deep into Kluane, but a few members of the Yukon legislature would like to change that. Years ago a proposal surfaced to build a loop road through the park. It would begin near park headquarters in Haines Junction, trace the Dezadeash River into the mountains, then the Kaskawulsh River north and west, and finally the Slims River back to the Alaska Highway—a total of about 60 miles.

"It would cost a fortune," Kluane park warden Lloyd Freese told us. "The area has dozens of surging glaciers, and rivers that flood and change course frequently. Landslides are common, too. I suspect parts of the road would wash out and have to be rebuilt often." Even then, it's doubtful that visitors would see the numbers of animals they see in Denali, since the road there primarily follows a broad tundra valley where animals migrate and gather to feed and to raise their young. The proposed road in Kluane, on the other hand, would follow turbulent rivers and skirt steep mountain slopes. Yet the debate continues, for Kluane, like Denali, struggles with the dichotomy of trying to protect a wilderness while at the same time providing for growing numbers of visitors.

The two parks have other similarities as well, one of them caribou. Not that either has a tremendous number of these nomads of the north; but situations in both focus attention on caribou and on the importance of understanding and protecting them.

"Only the wind knows the way of the caribou," say the Inuit people. Perhaps, then, only the wind knows why caribou populations rise and fall across Alaska and northern Canada. Several decades ago Adolph Murie estimated the Denali caribou herd at 20,000 to 30,000 animals. By 1977, aerial surveys, which Murie did not use, placed the number at 1,000. In more recent years it has increased to about 3,200. Why? No one is certain, but research has come up with some clues. Of 225 newborn calves collared in the Denali herd from 1984 to 1987, 89 (about 40 percent) died within the first 15 days of birth, and others died soon after. Of those 89 deaths, 87 were attributed to predation. Grizzly bears killed at least half; wolves at least a quarter. Even golden eagles and wolverines preyed on the calves, though not in large numbers. All this despite the fact that caribou calves can stand an hour after birth, run and swim three days later, double their weight in two weeks, and gain a hundred pounds in their first five months. Born into difficult odds, they embody the hard realities of the north.

Some years ago I was picking blueberries near Wonder Lake, in Denali, when suddenly a caribou bull appeared only 20 feet away. Never had I been so close to a caribou, or wanted to be. He snorted—not a good sign. I backed up and he stepped toward me—again, not a good sign. Despite my nervousness, I saw him as strikingly noble in his handsome pelage and velvet-cloaked antlers. Then he turned away and pranced over the tundra. Stopping at a small spruce, he raked his antlers along its trunk and branches, and by the time he finished velvet hung from his antlers in long shreds—and the spruce was devastated.

Seeing a single caribou in the wild can be memorable, but multiply it by a thousand, or 20 thousand, and you have one of the greatest wildlife spectacles in North America. You can witness such gatherings in several places across Alaska and Canada, for there are a number of caribou herds. But let's say it's one o'clock in the morning in early July on the North Slope of Alaska's Arctic National Wildlife Refuge, next door to Canada's North Yukon National Park, and you are awakened by the sound of hooves clicking on river gravel. Two hours earlier when you climbed into your tent and fell asleep, not a single caribou was in sight. Now, peering out, you see thousands.

These caribou belong to the Porcupine herd, so named for the Porcupine River, which flows through one of the herd's main wintering areas in the Yukon Territory. Every spring many of the 180,000 animals in this herd move west across the international boundary, which means nothing to them, and arrive here, on the North Slope of the Brooks Range, to calve near the Hulahula and Jago Rivers—an area where industry wants to drill for oil and natural gas.

Each caribou is a single organism, yet when seen moving in the thousands across the tundra in wild, poetic harmony, the entire herd becomes one organism as well. It's an awesome sight—a sight some would risk jeopardizing for a moderate supply of oil, essentially a short-term solution to a long-term problem. Yet for many who have seen caribou move over the arctic tundra, seen their breath backlit by glowing midnight light, and heard the sound of hooves like music on the land, the price is too high. The land up here doesn't bend, it breaks; industrial scars inflicted in a day can last for centuries. And the caribou, what would become of them? Ask the wind.

No caribou live year-round in Kluane, though two small herds frequent areas nearby. They are woodland caribou, larger and less migratory than the barren-ground species in Alaska and the northern Yukon. One of the herds frequents the Burwash Uplands, an area rich in alpine and subalpine habitat, and rich in minerals as well. When Kluane National Park Reserve was on the drawing boards in the early 1970s, the Burwash Uplands were included. But the miners complained, the caribou did not, and the uplands, considered by many to be some of the finest country in the area, were finally excluded from the park.

A
utumn was waning when park warden Lloyd Freese, Melanie, and I hiked the trail to St. Elias Lake at the southeastern end of Kluane. Bundled in wool hats and down vests, we set a fast pace and soon warmed up in the early winter air. Wind gusted down the mountains and stripped the aspens of their leaves. It felt good to be in that wind, among those trees, trekking a trail used by moose and bears as well as humans. It's not a long hike to St. Elias Lake, but long enough to leave behind the sounds of the highway. That was important, for I was feeling uncomfortably civilized; a bit like Huckleberry Finn, I suppose, looking to run away to a wilder world.

As we approached the lake, something caught Lloyd's eye. "Look at that," he said, pointing to a rugged 2,000-foot cliff that flanked the lake. "There's a mountain goat up there!" Melanie and I rolled our eyes. "No, I'm serious," Lloyd said. "There's a mountain goat up there." A somber sky obscured the upper reaches of the cliff. Clouds swirled in and out. Scanning the rock face with binoculars, I found it hard to imagine that anything could live up there.

Then I spied the goat—a small patch of white against a black wall of rock. It walked atop a fin-shaped ridge that appeared no wider than the animal itself. I could see its long, shaggy hair blowing in the wind, and noticeable, too, were its small black horns.

Lloyd, Melanie, and I fell silent. Clouds rolled in again and obscured our view. Snow squalls were brewing at the other end of the lake. When the clouds lifted 30 minutes later, we spotted the goat again, higher this time, walking a narrow ledge and stopping occasionally to graze. Its hooves enable a mountain goat to scale such heights. Each hoof is split into two toes; rough pads on the sole grip the ground, and the toes can spread wide for even firmer balance.

Mountain goats are not particular eaters. Living where they do, they can't afford to be. They prefer grasses but will feed on subalpine shrubs and low-growing conifers. Alpine ridges and meadows offer excellent summer grazing, and the goats roam there, but never far from cliffs that afford protection should a wolf, bear, or wolverine suddenly appear. Golden eagles, too, pose a threat, preying on newborn kids.

As if surviving the weather and predation weren't enough, the mountain goat, like nearly every other species of North American wildlife, has had to contend with human intrusions. In northern British Columbia, for example, seismic tests and mineral exploration have displaced the goats from their cliffs and alpine homes. An estimated 700 to 800 live in Kluane, most of them in the more temperate southern half of the park. Dall sheep, their closest ecological equivalent in Kluane, live in the northern part. Other species of wild sheep inhabit areas of North America, some as far south as the desert Southwest, but only one species of wild goat lives here. And if the truth be known, it's not a goat at all, but a mountain antelope more closely related to the chamois of Europe than to any mammal on this side of the Atlantic.

Lloyd took one last look at the shaggy goat. "It's amazing an animal can live up there like that," he said. "I doubt most people would last a day. I've been here for 17 years and I'm still impressed."

The snow squalls moved across the lake and hit us as we turned down the trail and walked away. It felt as though in one day autumn had ended and winter had begun. Melanie and I climbed into our car, Lloyd into his truck, each thankful for the warmth of the engine. After a day in the wind and cold, civilization began to sound appealing. We bade Lloyd farewell and drove out of Kluane National Park Reserve. Yet all the way home I thought of that mountain goat, up there alone amid the cliffs and the wind and the advent of winter.

Sipping hot tea at home four months later, I sat back and stared at the words on my computer monitor. The mercury outside stood at minus 15 degrees, colder than average for mid-January in Anchorage. Frost glazed the windows, and my eyes drifted away, my mind following, until I didn't see my computer any more but rather a solitary mountain goat on a rocky ledge, a grizzly track in the river mud, a band of Dall sheep on a windblown slope, and more, much more. The spell of the Yukon was still on me.

And when I drifted back home and looked again through the frosty window, a raven flew by and did a full barrel roll. □

FOLLOWING PAGES: *Autumn blaze of aspens fires the flatlands beneath the Kluane Ranges. More than 45 mammal species thrive amid the park's dramatic mix of peak and plain, forest and tundra, glacier and river.*

*Surefooted beyond its years, a young Dall ewe
(above) races down a gravelly mountainside while two
companions (opposite) playfully butt each other. Born in
May and June, lambs remain with adult ewes for at least
two years, then separate into male and female bands.*

*PAGES 160–161: A wolf pack's leader scans forested
slopes for prey. Superior intelligence and acute senses of
smell, sight, and hearing make wolves the northland's
consummate hunters, able to bring down moose and
caribou. Threatened elsewhere, wolves endure in areas like
Kluane, protected by law and by the land's remoteness.*

Papua
New Guinea:

Island Paradise of Birds

*Splendid in song and plumage, a common
paradise-kingfisher adds whistled trills to a rain
forest's avian chorus. New Guinea and its
neighboring islands are home to more than 700
known species of birds—more than in
all of Europe. This rich diversity exists primarily
because of the islands' great range of habitats.*

MICHAEL S. YAMASHITA

Text by Ron Fisher

Photographs by Michael S. Yamashita

W ith a feather in his hat, ornithologist Bruce Beehler led the way along a muddy trail in the rain forest of Papua New Guinea, a nation occupying the eastern half of the island of New Guinea off the northern coast of Australia. The trail climbed and fell as it crossed crests and ridges. Rainwater dripped on us from trailside bamboo, and a dove somewhere in the forest softly called *hoo hoo hoo.* We were looking for a tree, a particular tree, where the Count Raggi's bird of paradise—*Paradisaea raggiana*—comes to perform its frenzied and lustful dances.

We found the tree, a tall fig reaching well up into the canopy, and sat down at its base. Bruce was in Papua New Guinea to study its birds for the Smithsonian Institution in Washington, D.C. He had rigged a lean-to of blue plastic and under it had placed a battered lawn chair, its back tilted to a comfortable angle. His spotting scope, protruding through a hole in the plastic, was focused on the branches where the birds displayed. He spent a lot of time here, waiting for birds.

Toward the end of the afternoon the birds began to arrive—all males. Had we been looking down on them we'd have had a better view, for they had picked the leaves from the treetop branches to make themselves visible to passing females. Clearing a treetop also makes the birds vulnerable to attack from above. "The first one in risks getting taken by a hawk," Bruce said. "I've had four hawks attack in the month I've been here. The Raggis are here every day, and the hawks know it. For them, it's like going to McDonald's for a Big Mac. Some ornithologists have even speculated that that's why the Raggianas clear the leaves away: so they can see the hawks coming."

From our vantage on the ground we could see their lacy, rust-colored plumage through the leaves as the birds darted from limb to limb, occasionally trumpeting a raucous note skyward. One bowed his head, and his wings came up and the tips touched. His head dropped farther until it was between his feet. Then his deep red display plumes arched up and waved above his body. Soon the bird was joined by a second and a third, all calling and dancing together.

When a female—drab and diminutive—arrived, the males became frantic in their displaying, bowing deeply, hurling their red plumes over their heads, shouting *ki ki ki*, practically turning themselves inside out in their eagerness to look their best. The female hopped from branch to branch, watching. *Kuss kuss kuss* she scolded, evidently unmoved.

Réné P. Lesson of France was the first naturalist to see birds of paradise in the wild, in 1824. He reported that "a Paradisaea suddenly flew in graceful curves over my head. It was like a meteor whose body, cutting through the air, leaves a long trail of light."

Papua New Guinea—or PNG, as the locals call it—entered the 20th century later than many other parts of the world. Its rugged interior, home to malaria and headhunters, resisted final exploration until the 1930s or even later, and much of the writing about the country has dwelt on its affinity with the Stone Age. It's true, the first wheels some of the interior's aborigines saw were attached to airplanes, and the civilization that came down out of the sky onto them was so advanced, by their standards, as to be indistinguishable from magic.

But missionaries, prospectors, and Australian government officials have done their work. The country is pretty well civilized, though a striking duality still exists there: men in paint and feathers stepping out of helicopters; naked children splashing in rivers as tour boats chug by.

PNG is slightly larger than California and has a population of more than three million, about the same as Connecticut's. Most of the people live in isolated tribal villages in the interior and speak mutually unintelligible languages—some 700 of them, by most counts. Pidgin, a rollicking, simplified speech, is almost universally spoken and understood.

Rivers the color of creamed coffee meander across broad savannas that merge with rain forest-clothed mountains. Knifelike ridges, most with narrow trails running along them, bisect looming ranges that reach to 15,000 cloudy feet. And the skies and trees are filled with birds.

Birds. Birds have fascinated me for years. They are as mysterious and beguiling as any of earth's creatures. There are about 8,700 different kinds, of which more than 5,000 are songbirds and maybe 320 are parrots. Individual birds number perhaps 100 billion.

According to ornithologists James Fisher and Roger Tory Peterson, among others, birds do an impressive number of things by instinct: fight their way out of the egg, hide, flock and forage, scratch and preen, sing and cry, migrate, orient themselves and navigate, establish territories, display, and feed and protect their young. "Yet nearly all these activities can be, and often are, improved by experience, by learning." Practice makes a better bird.

Birds make a variety of sounds, either calls or songs. Calls communicate alarm, rally flocks, and intimidate enemies and competitors. Calls are for business, but songs are for love—or at least for reproduction. Songs establish territories, attract members of the opposite sex, synchronize sexual behavior, and strengthen the bond between mates. Songs of birds even in the same species can vary to such an extent that ornithologists speak of bird "dialects."

But, say Fisher and Peterson, "Birds talk as much with ritual movements of their bodies, with mime and dance, as with their voices." Which brings us back to Papua New Guinea, home to perhaps the most accomplished mimes and dancers in the whole world of birds.

New Guinea and its associated islands have more than 700 species of birds, about 100 fewer than in all of North America. Ornithologist Jared M. Diamond once recorded 108 species in a one-mile radius of a lowland rain forest near Madang. This avian richness derives largely from the great variety of habitats in New Guinea. There are coral atolls and tropical rain forests, dry woodland savannas and cold upland forests, high mountain grasslands and snowcapped mountaintops. The birds have divided up this terrain in a wonderfully efficient manner. Every species has a niche.

I journeyed to New Guinea one recent summer and, carefully marking my checklist, tallied 145 of the island's species in about four weeks of amateur birding.

My first stop was an area slightly off the beaten path even in PNG. The Tonda Wildlife Management Area covers 54 square miles in the far southwestern corner of the country, where the Bensbach River flows into the Arafura Sea. It's a landscape reminiscent of African savannas: broad grasslands punctuated by palms and fig trees silhouetted against huge clouds sliding across the sky. Rusa deer, introduced by Dutch missionaries in 1922, and wallabies, reminders of the nearness of Australia, graze on the seas of grasses. A comfortable lodge, catering largely to fishermen who come to try the barramundi-rich waters of the Bensbach, served as headquarters for photographer Mike Yamashita and me. From there we ventured up and down the river in a flat-bottomed boat in quest of birds, assisted by a local guide named Sinakai.

It was the high-water season, and the river had left its banks, creating in many places vast shallow lakes where water birds waded and fed. Rows of trees and bushes marked the course of the meandering river. From its banks flocks of black-and-white magpie geese lifted off. Pelicans waddled about and preened themselves with their huge pink bills. Birds were everywhere. You didn't need to look for one; you simply peered through your binoculars and took your pick. At one point there were six species in my field of view: royal spoonbill, with a spatula-shaped bill; great egret; masked lapwing; pied heron; glossy ibis; and Australian pelicans as somber as jurists. The spoonbill looked as if it needed a bath, but the glossy ibis was (Continued on page 170)

Dazzling lesser bird of paradise performs a nuptial display. Magellan's men may have brought back plumes of this species to Spain. Europeans believed such birds were celestial, soaring in perpetual flight, feeding on dew.

Iridescent breast shield, golden whiskers, and six wirelike crown plumes mark a Carola's parotia, a bird of paradise rarely seen. Tribesmen seeking such exotic feathers invoke aid from ancestral ghosts. At right, a hunter aims a forked arrow designed to limit damage to skins of avian prey.

as sleek as a Stealth Bomber. The lapwings, with large, yellow facial wattles, were noisy and belligerent. They feed, according to my copy of *Birds of New Guinea*, "in typical plover fashion (walk-peck-walk)."

Sinakai enjoyed looking through my bird book. He was very knowledgeable about birds and could spot them long before I could. His huge, gnarled finger would point to a bird's picture. "This fella, plenty here," he would say. I asked him what was the prettiest bird along the Bensbach. "Jacana," he replied. Later we saw one, a long-legged wader with a bright red comb, walking on floating vegetation. The jacana may have the longest toes of any bird its size and always walks, never hops.

A white-bellied sea-eagle, whose call is a metallic clank, drifted overhead, and in the distance a brolga, a large gray crane, stood foraging in shallow water, probing with its bill. Little pied cormorants sat atop dead snags.

Sinakai spotted three Papuan frogmouths in a hoary fig tree on the bank. Two of them were cuddling, the head of one resting on the back of the other's neck. Big owl-like birds, frogmouths hunt at night and perch during the day on large branches, immobile. Their mottled feathers blend with the trees. The birds sit with their beaks pointed skyward, which gives them a smug, snooty look. Later I would hear the frogmouth's voice, a low steady humming, *ommmm*, like a Hare Krishna's.

We pulled the boat into a sort of lagoon rimmed by bushy vegetation and sat quietly for a while. Soon a shining flycatcher with delicate whiskers and a cool, rapid trill was busy in the understory, and a pale blue kingfisher patrolled the riverbank, diving for fish and crabs. Another flycatcher sat on a perch, restlessly sweeping its tail from side to side. A relative of the kingfisher, a blue-winged kookaburra came and perched, too. Its enormous head looked too big for its body. It would sit motionless on a branch, then descend to gulp down a crab or a frog. The kookaburra's voice, says my field guide, sounds "somewhat like a machine-driven hacksaw."

The sounds along the river were astounding: warbles, gurgles, chirps, and whistles; honks and shrieks and hoots and crackles; moans and groans and raucous catcalls; loud calls, soft calls, tiny cheeps, and cowlike bellows.

One day Sinakai and his partner, Tapari, took us to the mouth of the river, an overnight trip of some 60 miles. Our little boat pounded along in the hot sun as my knees turned pink. At the mouth, there were mud and mangrove thickets and a wide, empty sky above the ocean. It was an abandoned and spooky place. People from nearby Irian Jaya, part of Indonesia, come here, Sinakai said, "to steal the crocodiles." On the banks, little bugs and hoppers and tiny, primitive, slithery creatures made tracks in the gray mud. Mosquitoes swarmed around us. It was a relief to head back upstream.

We camped beside a favored fishing hole and dined on catfish from the river, cooked on a bed of palm leaves over an open fire, and chicken brought from the lodge. With nothing but a machete and nimble fingers, Tapari made a bow and arrow from bamboo and palm leaves and went wallaby hunting. Varied trillers foraged for caterpillars and fruit in the canopy, slurring *breer breer breer*. Three white-headed stilts waded in the shallows on spindly red legs. They barked like puppies: *kyap kyap kyap*. Wild pigs loped across the meadow with a rocking-horse gait.

I made my bed beneath a wall of black palms, with the Southern Cross above my feet. A meteor streaked across the sky, the largest and brightest I'd ever seen, a fireball trailing sparks. As I drifted off to sleep, I could hear Sinakai and Tapari, one generation removed from the days of the headhunters, sharpening their machetes by the fire.

On the north coast of Papua New Guinea, the Sepik River, renowned for the wood carvings of the people who live along it, empties into the Bismarck Sea. Up one of its tributaries, the Karawari, there's another lodge in the heart of rich bird habitat in the foothills of the Central Range. In the mornings there you wake to a monotonous chorus of friarbirds or the froglike croakings of yellow-faced mynahs. Flocks of parrots fly back and forth across the river. Egrets and herons are common, and Brahminy kites, large, fierce-looking raptors with beautiful white heads, perch in dead trees at the forest's edge. In late afternoon palm cockatoos and hornbills wing over the water.

Our guide on the Karawari was Chris—Christopheles Karimban—another knowledgeable local birder. He had his own well-thumbed copy of *Birds of New Guinea* and was a master at spotting the various species. He laughed with delight at their antics—an egret hunting, for instance—and could imitate many. Ornithologist Steven Feld found that among the area's Kaluli people virtually all the men could sit before his tape recorder and identify at least a hundred birds just from their sounds. The Kaluli had more trouble describing the birds' physical characteristics. One, exasperated with Feld's questions, said, "Listen—to you they are birds, to me they are voices in the forest."

The voices came to us out of the forest, from across the river, and off lakes. Chris took us one day upstream a few miles to Yimas Lakes—a series of still, shallow, interconnected bodies of water where birds flock.

We stopped along the way at a couple of dusty villages, small collections of palm-and-bamboo houses built on poles. The people, though among the fiercest-looking on earth, were shy and friendly. They grinned with pleasure when I caught their eye. Some of the young ones knew a few words of English. They barely whispered when they spoke; I had to lean forward to hear them. Children would touch me softly with their cool, dry hands, as if to make sure I was real. Many of their parents had carvings for sale, of crocodiles and birds. One village had a pet cockatoo named Cocky, bad-tempered and noisy. In another, a pair of young cassowaries, about two feet tall and a scruffy brown, had the run of the place. Cassowaries grow up to be big, ostrich-like birds, valued for their meat and feathers—and, like pigs, as a sign of wealth. They're elusive in the wild, where they're hunted with bows and arrows.

On the river, little boys of five or six paddled their own canoes, miniature versions of their fathers'. Others squealed as they slid down shiny mud slides into the water—water, incidentally, in which a few crocodiles still lurk. Cormorants and white-winged black terns sat on dead branches. (When Chris pointed out a tern to me, he wouldn't say simply, "Tern." He would say, "White-winged black tern." There are about 15 species of terns in PNG alone.) We got a glimpse of a pair of Victoria crowned pigeons, big terrestrial gray-and-maroon birds with spectacular fan-shaped crests.

At Yimas Lakes a family from the village was hunting ducks: mother in the stern of the canoe, paddling; young son in the middle, along for the ride; father standing up front with his bow and arrows. We watched as they crept up on flocks of whistling tree ducks that were diving in the shallows. The archer shot into the air at a steep angle so that the arrows would fall nearly straight down among the feeding birds. He never quite hit one; I think both the hunter and the hunted were made nervous by spectators.

The birds of New Guinea, like those elsewhere, were once hunted more fiercely and more efficiently to supply the feather trade. As a 17th-century New England clergyman, William Morrell, noted in a poem about birds, "With these sweete dainties man is sweetly fed, / With these rich feathers ladies plume their head. . . ." From about the mid-1800s to early in the 20th century, feathers were popular adornments on women's hats. Bird preservationists estimated that by 1900 some 200 million birds were being killed each year for their feathers and skins. Of these, perhaps 80,000 were birds of paradise from New Guinea and nearby islands. Between 1904 and 1908, 155,000 bird of paradise skins were auctioned in London.

The extinction of the passenger pigeon in the wild by 1900 helped preservationists marshal public opinion against the traffic in bird skins, and by the second decade of this century both the U.S. and the United Kingdom had legislation forbidding their importation. Since 1924, no birds of paradise have been legally collected for commercial purposes anywhere in New Guinea.

Two other things helped save birds of paradise: the tremendous extent of their forest habitat, and their mating behavior. Only full-grown males had valuable plumage, and were thus in danger of being taken, yet females would readily mate with drab young males—which were always in plentiful supply.

In 1522 Ferdinand Magellan's men had introduced bird of paradise skins to Europe. As their legs had been cut off to facilitate shipping, the legend arose that the birds never perched, but instead flew constantly through paradise feeding on dew. The legend didn't survive, but the name stuck, at least for the greater bird of paradise—*Paradisaea apoda*, footless bird of paradise.

New Guinea has 38 widely dissimilar kinds of birds of paradise. British naturalist David Attenborough says, "The birds of paradise, in fact, are alike only in that their plumage is of almost unbelievable extravagance and they indulge in ecstatic courtship dances during which they display their glorious plumes to drab hens."

One of the best places in PNG to see birds of paradise is 7,000 feet up in the Southern Highlands at Tari Gap—a notch in the mountains with a road running through it. About 150 species of birds have been recorded here, including 10 birds of paradise. Walk along the road and you're likely to see perhaps 20 pygmy lorikeets chattering as they hang upside down in a tree, feeding on figs. Nearby in a casuarina tree are maybe 50 rainbow lorikeets, which *Birds of New Guinea* calls "the nearly ubiquitous NG parrot."

Every 50 feet I am stopped to be shown a bird I have never seen before. A brown sicklebill with an enormously long tail flits by. Its long, downward curving bill is as distinctive as its tail. During World War II, when Japanese and Allied troops fought over New Guinea, soldiers sometimes opened fire in the direction of this bird when they heard its call, remarkably like a burst of machine gun fire. Bruce Beehler has noted that sicklebill males pay an ironic price for their elaborate courtship displays: "The male is forced to stay near his display tree, singing to attract mates, and courting the females that visit him there. The female is free to wander. . . ."

Wild dogs howl deep in the forest. A ribbon-tailed astrapia comes by. It has lost its tail; it should be trailing a long white ribbon. A helicopter pilot I talked with remembers seeing ribbon-tails coming up out of the trees toward him "like rockets."

Glossy swiftlets fly back and forth overhead. They nest here in overhanging road cuts and sheltered rock faces. Friendly fantails—that's their name, friendly fantails—are common. They spread their tails in a perky way as they perch. The wings of Papuan mountain pigeons make a whistling sound as the birds pass overhead. Pied chats sit nervously in the grasslands flicking their wings. Even several kinds of robins are present. Smoky honeyeaters are as common as crows; they are nondescript except for conspicuous yellow eye patches. A short walk down from the saddle of the gap I see a superb bird of paradise—again, that's its name, superb. Its chest is covered by an iridescent blue wedge-shaped shield that cannot be retracted. It's an astonishing bird that my field guide calls "common."

As late afternoon fog comes rolling in, a King of Saxony bird of paradise flies from tree to tree, its long, pearly blue head plumes trailing behind it. It sits and shakes its plumes and utters its call, a noise like radio static. In local folklore the King of Saxony is said to have stolen its plumes from a grassland bird and gone to hide in the forest. Naturalists knew the King of Saxony species existed for 50 years before a complete specimen was collected: The birds' plumes had been showing up in shipments of feathers for the fashion industry.

Earlier I had come across a sentence in *Birds* *(Continued on page 179)*

Motorized dugout skims
past thick rain forest on the
Karawari River, habitat of
abundant bird life. Dawn
highlights gregarious
Australian pelicans (below)
along the bank of a stream.

FOLLOWING PAGES: A flock
of migrating royal spoonbills
rests and feeds in the Tonda
Wildlife Management Area,
refuge for more than 200
species of birds.

of New Guinea that had intrigued me. Concerning wood-swallows: "Parties have the distinctive habit of perching side-by-side on a branch, with the bodies of adjacent birds pressed together." On the road through Tari Gap I saw eight of these little birds, all white but for their black heads, scrunched up in a row on an exposed branch. They weren't just touching; they were *squeezed* together, their white bodies merging into one big body with eight heads. They made me think of a bed full of children with their heads sticking out of the covers.

The valley below Tari Gap has its own bird life, and I went there one day to a casuarina tree in which half a dozen Count Raggi's birds of paradise were displaying. A little boy in ragged shorts led me closer to the tree, through a tidy garden of sweet potatoes and sugarcane. I showed him a picture of a Raggi in my field guide. "Aieee!" he cried, taken aback. He paged through the book and came to a white cockatoo. He looked up at me with serious brown eyes. "Cocky," he said. I showed him how to use my binoculars, and he rocked back and forth on his heels as he focused.

Sadly, the young people of Papua New Guinea are losing interest in their birds, according to Bruce Beehler. "Probably 80 percent of the PNG high school students have never seen a bird of paradise and wouldn't know where to go to see one. The people are getting farther and farther removed from their wildlife."

As well as birds of paradise, Papua New Guinea has bowerbirds. Naturalist E. Thomas Gilliard wrote: "It is perhaps not too much to say that paradise birds are the most beautiful of all living creatures and that, short of man himself, bower birds are the most bizarre. . . . A nineteenth century naturalist once suggested that just as mammals are commonly divided into two groups—man and the lower forms—all birds should be split into two categories: bower birds and other birds."

New Guinea has 11 known species of bowerbirds. Describing their remarkable behavior, Gilliard goes on to say: ". . . the males of some species build elaborate walled bowers of sticks and decorate them with bright objects and even with paint. Others construct towers up to nine feet high, some with tepee-like roofs and internal chambers, on circular lawns that they tend carefully and embellish with golden resins, garishly coloured berries, iridescent insect skeletons and fresh flowers that are replaced as they wither."

The satin bowerbird paints its bower, making dye by mixing charcoal, bits of fruit, and saliva, and using a small piece of bark as a brush.

Elusive forest giant, a northern cassowary may measure five feet in height. The flightless bird uses its bony crest to push its way through undergrowth. Normally timid, it will kick savagely with its clawed feet when threatened.

The streaked bowerbird builds a hut-shaped bower of many thousands of sticks. The hut has two entrances and, in front, a yard with a garden of moss where the bird daily puts fresh flowers and fruit.

The males of these species perform their passionate dances in front of their bowers, and the females, bedazzled by both the builders and the buildings, come to watch. What female could resist such ardor?

We heard of a yellow-breasted bowerbird's bower in the valley and went to find it. Two men of the Huli tribe, whose land we were on, led the way through tangled undergrowth to the base of a tree, where the bird had cleared the forest floor of every leaf and twig. He had flown away when he heard us coming, so in an effort to lure him back one of the men sprinkled a few leaves on the floor of his bower. Compulsive tidiers, the birds can't resist restoring order; but though we sat quietly in the forest for an hour or so, our bird didn't return.

In the same area we went in quest of the blue bird of paradise, arguably the most beautiful bird in the world. The male is a little larger than a starling, with a white bill, white eye-rings, black hood, and blue back. His frilly plumes are not long, but his two black tail streamers hang down a foot or so. When displaying, he hangs by his feet upside down. "Viewed from the front, the plumes, inconspicuous and rather disappointing when at rest, form a brilliant, inverted triangle, with the raised feathers of the abdomen completing the center," ornithologist L. S. Crandall wrote. "In the middle appears a . . . patch of velvet black, bordered above by a narrow band of dull red, formed by the feathers that ordinarily clothe the abdomen. The long, pendant 'wires' rise to half their length, then droop gracefully downward on either side. The wings are held tightly closed and the head is turned upward. During the display, the body is moved forward and back . . . and with a violent motion of the body the plumage is frequently spread to its widest expanse." Another ornithologist, C. R. Stoner, observed that the "colour-effects produced are truly marvellous, slight movements of the plumes causing shimmering waves of blue and violet to pass across the fan. . . ."

Little boys led us through the slippery fields and gardens at the forest's edge—mounds of neatly tilled taro, sago, pineapples, beans, and sugarcane. We heard the occasional call of a blue bird of paradise—slow, plaintive down-slurs: *Whar. Whar. Whar.* The children were intrigued by our interest in birds and, once they got the hang of it, pointed to every bird they saw. Finally we caught up with a blue bird of paradise, and I captured it for a moment in my binoculars: blue frills and long black dangles, a calm and graceful settling, a quick white eye, and a sudden flurried departure.

It was here in the Wahgi Valley and in the hills around Tari Gap that I began to understand better the significance of birds in the life of the tribal people of Papua New Guinea. Because of the ruggedness of the terrain, customs vary widely from culture to culture and even from village to village; a ritual important to one group may be unknown to the people across the ridge. Still, in nearly all the cultures, birds play a prominent and complex role.

In some cultures the local name of the Count Raggi's bird of paradise is invoked in chants to make children beautiful. The Huli people greatly admire the industry of the bowerbird. They will burn a few twigs from a bower, cook taro over the fire, then smear the taro on the bodies of their children to make them industrious. Similarly, when they make a drum, they burn a feather from the blue bird of paradise and blow its ashes onto the drum to invest it with the steady and powerful sound of the bird's call.

The Kaluli people never kill the birds in the trees nearest their villages, believing them to be the spirits of friends and relatives who have died. The Kaluli also believe that the three descending notes of the white-crowned koel say "My back hurts," a reference to the bird's nearly constant flying. Another bird's plaintive song is thought to be the cry of a lost or abandoned boy. Kaluli do not feed their children birds that live on the ground, lest they grow up unable to walk properly.

Ornithologist Steven Feld spent some time with the Kaluli and found that their days are enriched by the sounds of the forest. They waken to the trilling of kingfishers and the hooting of a distant coucal. "Whistlers, friarbirds, and grackles amplify the dawn." During the day, the people chop firewood and work in their gardens, with the sounds of birds everywhere. They whistle and sing with them, to them, about them. They make up songs about the sounds they hear. "Kaluli sing like the forest, in overlapping layers." Cicadas add their sounds as the men fell a tree, and a Kaluli song imitates the constant swarming noise of the insects. After a late afternoon rain shower, orioles, birds of paradise, and friarbirds call from the bush. In the evening frogs and insects are heard, and nightjars and owls signal another night.

In the 1970s Ian Saem Majnep, a native of eastern Papua New Guinea, wrote *Birds of My Kalam Country* with anthropologist Ralph Bulmer. If you dream about long-tailed birds of paradise, Majnep reported, you are dreaming about women, for the plumes are black and brown, the colors of women, and the plumes are also like a woman's skirt. If you shoot a long-tailed bird whose feathers have been damaged, it means the bird knew it was going to die and deliberately spoiled its own plumage. The mountain pigeon is cooked in oven pits in new taro gardens to propitiate the ghosts of ancestors who had previously farmed there. If a willie wagtail comes to a new garden and sings *jt jt*, the crops will flourish. Newlyweds will not eat mannikins because those birds "have big families, and newly married people don't want to have a whole lot of children very fast." And if you go into a banana garden after eating a harpy-eagle, the young banana shoots will wither and die; the eagle's claws have grasped and killed them.

But even more important than the rituals, taboos, and lore of birds in Papua New Guinea are the uses of birds and their feathers in costume and dance. Anthropologist Kenneth E. Read writes that New Guinea

181

"is a huge 'aviary' for a species whose contrived plumage rivals the birds that flash like vivid thoughts through the vaults of the jungle."

Papua New Guinea men decorate themselves, according to anthropologists Andrew and Marilyn Strathern, "to astonish, delight, and attract women." The women raise the young children, tend the gardens, and look after the pigs. So the men have little to do but engage in complex social rituals—rituals that often involve the exchange of valuable gifts or periodic displays of wealth. It is at these ceremonies, as well as at dances called sing-sings, that they decorate themselves.

I watched a group of Spirit Dancers prepare to perform at a lodge near Tari Gap. Nearly naked, they gathered on a lawn outside the lodge to decorate themselves. They were Huli wigmen, so each had a large wig made of human hair and shaped like Napoleon's hat. They used little pieces of broken mirror to apply their paint—red, yellow, and black. Into the hair of their wigs they stuck the feathers of birds. An ornithologist from the San Diego Zoo once counted the feathers of 28 species of birds in one Huli wig. David Attenborough met a Huli man whose headdress contained plumes from at least 30 individual birds of paradise belonging to 5 different species.

The feathers were carefully removed from their storage places between graying pieces of cardboard. "These feathers are treasured, hoarded, traded, and often are used year after year and passed on from one generation to the next," Bruce Beehler has written. Some bird feathers are more valuable than others. The blue bird of paradise feathers are the rarest and the most eagerly bartered for. The shield of the superb bird of paradise is worn on the forehead, the seat of wisdom. Every element in a headdress transfers some aspect of a bird to its wearer.

The men delicately helped one another with their feathers and paint. As they worked, they sang snatches of song. "When men chant their beauty-magic before dressing up for dancing," wrote Majnep, "they call the names of all these birds, and of the trees at which they feed, and also the names of three cool green plants which grow by streamsides and in the forest. . . ." From the woods behind the men came the calls of birds and from overhead the whistle of the wings of even more birds. Birds above and birds below.

A dancer in full regalia is a sight to behold: a burly black man, bearded and fierce-looking, with cassowary feathers and rust-colored bird of paradise plumes reaching high above his head, and smaller feathers—even the entire bodies of small birds—adorning his wig or his hair. Paint in intricate patterns completes the decoration.

In the fairly recent past, bloody fighting between tribes and clans in Papua New Guinea was commonplace. Beginning in the 1950s, an effort was made to bring peoples from different tribes together peacefully, and the highland shows were born. A huge success from the start, there is now one every year at Mount Hagen and another at Goroka.

Thousands of tribal sing-sing groups come, put on their finest paint and feathers, and sing and dance in huge open fields. More thousands come to enjoy the spectacle, and in 1989 I was among them.

With other sunburned tourists I took refuge in the roofed grandstand at Mount Hagen as the show began. Late in the morning, from far down at one end of the arena—an open space the size of several football fields—came the sounds of drums and commotion. A group of performers entered, dancing and singing. Other groups followed, until the arena was filled with nearly three dozen—each costumed distinctively, each adding its own distinctive song and dance, all drumming and chanting together to produce a hypnotic spectacle and din. Thousands of performers took part, and acres of feathers swayed and bobbed as they danced. Nearly all the dancers were men, though a few groups were composed of women and a few others had women mixed in.

Most of the dances had some significance: reenactments of pig-killing festivals or historical incidents or courtship rituals. Many borrowed behavior from birds. Dark-barred feathers of male eagles, goura pigeons, cuckoo-doves, or hawks symbolized masculinity. Some men wore black cassowary feathers in their headdresses and reddish Count Raggi's feathers above their elbows; their dancing mimicked the movements of those birds. Another group stomped the ground fiercely as they danced, which made the King of Saxony feathers in their headdresses sway as they do when the bird performs its courtship display.

With my binoculars I scanned the performers. They were rapt, their oiled and painted bodies glistening in the sun. They wore sicklebill and astrapia feathers, Princess Stephanie feathers, feathers of cockatoos, parrots, lorikeets, red and blue birds of paradise, parotia plumes, and breast shields from superb birds of paradise. It was like seeing all the bird of paradise species come to life, come together, and dance their highly charged and strangely beautiful dances.

And there at Mount Hagen I perceived the harmony of the story. In the world of birds, the male of the species is the gaudy one, while the female is usually drab and shy. Papua New Guinea has the world's gaudiest birds, and celebrants use costume and dance to mimic them. With imagination, with feathers and paint and song, the men of this hidden world emerge from their forests to dance and sing, to celebrate their lives, to turn themselves into birds. □

FOLLOWING PAGES: Mist veils the Tari Basin, upland home of the Huli, a people unknown to outsiders until 1935. The male-dominated Huli culture values birds and other forest wildlife for use in rituals and adornment.

Warmed by a fire day and night, a thatched hut shelters a Huli mother and children. Men and older boys in this highland area usually live apart in more elaborate houses.

Preparing for a ritual, a Huli man preens his bird of paradise plumes. Cuscus fur and daisies decorate his human-hair wig. Feathers are often treasured heirlooms.

Bare branch and bright sunlight form a favored arena for the Count Raggi's bird of paradise. Males congregate in treetops to court females with showy song and dance. Head down, a Raggiana displays fiery, gossamer flank plumes (opposite). Widespread in Papua New Guinea, this species has been incorporated in the government's official seal.

Like exotic male birds
in courtship displays,
feathered dancers in
a sing-sing group
perform in the annual
highland show at Mount
Hagen. Such festivals
peacefully bring together
formerly warring tribes
and help preserve Papuan
cultural traditions.

Notched beak of a Blyth's hornbill decorates
a Huli wigman's back. The headdress of the
Wahgi woman at right includes entire
birds. She wears necklaces of cowrie shells.

PAGES 194–195: Painted and plumed,
Huli wigmen beat **kundus**, drums made of
snakeskin stretched over hollowed wood.

NOTES ON CONTRIBUTORS

In the early 1970s ROBERT CAPUTO rescued an orphaned chimpanzee in the rain forest of Zaire. His efforts to return the chimp to the wild led him to Tanzania's Ngorongoro Crater, where he worked on films for the TV series *Jane Goodall and the World of Animal Behavior*. He then spent three years on his own recording African wildlife on film. A native of North Carolina and a graduate of New York University's film school, Bob has been photographing and writing articles for NATIONAL GEOGRAPHIC since 1980.

BILL CURTSINGER began his photographic career in the 1960s as a member of a U.S. Navy diving unit. Since then he has survived a shark attack in the western Pacific, swum with whales in three oceans, and come face-to-face with dangerous leopard seals in polar waters. Now based in Portland, Maine, he is one of few photographers to have worked under both Arctic and Antarctic ice. Bill has undertaken assignments for National Geographic since 1970 on subjects ranging from dolphins and walruses to underwater archaeology.

A lifelong resident of New York City, DAVID DOUBILET began photographing underwater off New Jersey when he was 12. Over the past 20 years he has documented marine life in the Red Sea and the Caribbean, in the western Pacific and Hawaii, off Australia, New Guinea, and Baja California, and in British Columbia's Strait of Georgia; all are represented in his 1989 book *Light in the Sea*. A contract photographer for National Geographic since 1977, David always works with his wife, photographer and diver Anne Levine Doubilet.

With her chapter on Etosha, CHRISTINE ECKSTROM marks her third journey to Africa for Special Publications. Since joining the National Geographic staff in 1974, she has written about the East African grasslands for *Our Awesome Earth* and the Rift Valley region for *Excursion to Enchantment*. "The experience of being among the animals in the African bush is both exhilarating and humbling," she says. Other assignments have taken Chris to the Virgin Islands, Polynesia, the Seychelles, Indonesia, and the Philippines.

RON FISHER, from Iowa, has been writing or editing for National Geographic since 1967. He is the author of *Still Waters, White Waters* and two books about the Appalachian Trail, as well as several children's books on wildlife and chapters in many other Special Publications. His award-winning book *Our Threatened Inheritance* addressed issues surrounding national parks, forests, wildlife refuges, and other federal lands from Maine to Hawaii. Ron is currently writing about America's heartland for Special Publications.

Born and reared in the Pacific Northwest, free-lance writer and photographer KIM HEACOX has lived in Alaska for more than a decade. He says he could spend a lifetime exploring that state and the neighboring Yukon, where "deep respect and constant vigilance" are required to preserve the land and its wildlife. A former National Park Service ranger and biologist, Kim has contributed articles to NATIONAL GEOGRAPHIC TRAVELER as well as *Audubon, Wilderness, National Wildlife,* and *Nature Conservancy* magazines.

As a youngster growing up in northern Wisconsin, STEPHEN J. KRASEMANN went on trout-fishing trips with his grandfather, who encouraged him to explore the woods. Those excursions led to an abiding fascination with wildlife. A free lance now living in South Gillies, Ontario, Stephen has taken photographs for NATIONAL GEOGRAPHIC, TRAVELER, and other Society publications. He is currently working on a book about the Nature Conservancy and its preserves, and another entitled *Diary of an Arctic Year*.

A native Midwesterner, THOMAS O'NEILL joined the National Geographic staff in 1976. He is the author of *Back Roads America* and *Lakes, Peaks, and Prairies*, a book about the U.S.–Canadian border, and has written chapters for many other Special Publications, most recently *The World's Wild Shores*. Of the biologists he traveled with in the American tropics, Tom says, "Always in the back of their minds is the notion that they will discover something totally new. Their excitement makes even the shortest hike an adventure."

A free-lance photographer living in Mendham, New Jersey, MICHAEL S. YAMASHITA has contributed to Society publications since 1979, traveling to Japan and Somalia for NATIONAL GEOGRAPHIC and collaborating with Tom O'Neill on *Lakes, Peaks, and Prairies*. Among his current projects is a book called *In the Japanese Garden*. Mike considers his assignment to photograph the spectacular birds and tribal dancers of New Guinea to be one of the most exciting of his career.

ACKNOWLEDGMENTS

The Special Publications Division is grateful to the individuals named or quoted in the text and to those cited here for their generous assistance during the preparation of this book: Layne Adams, Jim Barry, Benjamin B. Beck, Eirik A.T. Blom, Doreen Brumley, Bob Butterfield, Ronald I. Crombie, Glenn Elison, Manfred Hoefs, Ron Larson, Ralph Lloyd, Tom Meier, Edward C. Murphy, Franklin D. Ross, Brian Slough, Victor Springer, Flip Stander, and Paul Swart.

Library of Congress CIP Data

Hidden worlds of wildlife / prepared by the Special Publications Division, National Geographic Society.
    p.   cm.
    Includes index.
    ISBN 0-87044-791-2
    1. Zoology. 2. Marine biology. I. National Geographic Society (U.S.). Special Publications Division.
QL45.2.H5   1990
591—dc20   90-13348
                                  CIP

Index

ADDITIONAL READING

The reader may wish to consult the *National Geographic Index* for related articles and books. The following books may also be of special interest. General: David Attenborough, *Life on Earth.* Etosha: Anthony Bannister and Peter Johnson, *Namibia: Africa's Harsh Paradise;* Michael Brittan, *Discover Namibia;* Mitch and Margot Reardon, *Etosha: Life & Death on an African Plain.* American Tropics: Adrian Forsyth and Ken Miyata, *Tropical Nature: Life and Death in the Rain Forests of Central and South America;* John C. Kricher, *A Neotropical Companion;* Peter C. H. Pritchard, *Encyclopedia of Turtles.* Ocean Worlds: David Doubilet, *Light in the Sea;* John May, *The Greenpeace Book of Antarctica.* Kluane: W. R. Hamilton, *The Yukon Story;* Adolph Murie, *A Naturalist in Alaska;* Robert W. Service, *Collected Poems.* Papua New Guinea: Bruce M. Beehler et al., *Birds of New Guinea;* Brian Miller, *The Highlands of Papua New Guinea;* Austin L. Rand and E. Thomas Gilliard, *Handbook of New Guinea Birds;* Andrew and Marilyn Strathern, *Self-Decoration in Mount Hagen;* Tony Wheeler, *Papua New Guinea: A Travel Survival Guide.*

Composition for this book by the Typographic section of National Geographic Production Services, Pre-Press Division. Set in Palatino. Printed and bound by R. R. Donnelley & Sons, Willard, Ohio. Color separations by Graphic Art Service, Inc., Nashville, Tenn.; Lanman Progressive Co., Washington, D.C.; Lincoln Graphics, Inc., Cherry Hill, N.J.; and NEC, Inc., Nashville, Tenn. Dust jacket printed by Federated Lithographers-Printers, Inc., Providence, R.I.